MW00676251

PRAISE FOR JOHN BURBIDGE

The Boatman: An Indian Love Story

Touching, honest, and brave, *The Boatman* draws us irresistibly into an intense new world. Vivid descriptions and a heady pace never let the reader go.
Dianne Highbridge, author of *A Much Younger Man* and *In the Empire of Dreams*

Burbidge's book is immensely educative and should be compulsory reading on how a foreigner discovers his true nature but returns home a very strong and confident man in charge of his life. *The Boatman* will surely take you across the Ganga.
Ashok Row Kavi, *Hindustan Times*

Those of us gay men who survived the eighties were all 'boatmen'. Burbidge's memoir allows us to remember and wonder.
Jeremy Fisher, author of *How to Tell Your Father to Drop Dead* and *Music from Another Country*

Unexpectedly contemporaneous, while still managing to evoke the ethos of a country in flux—the early profusion of exotica giving way to a more observed understanding of India.
Vikram Phukan, *TimeOut Mumbai*

While most urban gay men in 80s India might have fantasized about going to explore their sexuality in the West, Burbidge stumbles upon the reverse journey, which he tells with great honesty ... It would have been easier to write an exciting book about a foreigner's adventures in India. This is nuanced and ends up being all the more touching for it.
Sandip Roy, *Firstpost.com*

For a country that still criminalizes homosexuality, *The Boatman* chronicles its own cities that defy the law every night as spaces morph, people emerge and all types of liaisons are made and broken.
Priyanka Kotamraju, *The Hindu*

A charming account of an unspoken side of life in Mumbai in the 80s. Its strength lies in its unique perspective. Instead of coming out to his mother, Burbidge seems to come out to India.
Mahesh Dattani, playwright, director & actor

Burbidge took shocking risks in exploring his newfound homosexuality and found a capacity for the covert that both fascinated and appalled him. Along with his compassionate and respectful depiction of Indian street life from the perspective of an outsider with a keen eye for detail and a hunger for discovery, this makes for a memorable read. Highly recommended.
Jen Banyard, author of *Spider Lies, Mystery at Riddle Gully* and *Riddle Gully Runaway*

Dare Me! The Life and Work of Gerald Glaskin

John Burbidge's biography is one of the best yet written about an Australian writer.
David Hough, *The West Australian*

Burbidge has done us a favor in bringing an important writer back to the spotlight, and recounting a life that reveals much about marginality in twentieth century Australia.
Dennis Altman, author of *Homosexual: Oppression and Liberation*

A grand story masterfully told. His management of detail is one of its strengths—quite an amazing accomplishment.
Robert Dessaix, writer and critic

This impressive research brings Glaskin back from near oblivion. Burbidge gives us Glaskin with all his charm as well as his furious obstinacy.
Jeremy Fisher, *The Australian Book Review*

Vividly presented in the many circumstances of a warring but productive life, Glaskin has well merited Burbidge's entertaining and scrupulous attention.
Peter Pierce, *The Weekend Australian*

John Burbidge's biography rescues Glaskin from obscurity and uses his life to throw light on a period of Australian history that is attracting more and more attention.
Graham Willett, President, *Australian Lesbian and Gay Archives*

The sensitivity, respect and understanding Burbidge has brought to Glaskin's life and work is enormous. No doubt Glaskin would have berated or corrected Burbidge, but he could not help but have been proud and grateful to be so well understood and so generously described.
Jo Darbyshire, Curator, *The Gay Museum*, Western Australia

THE BOATMAN

AN INDIAN LOVE STORY

Also by John Burbidge

Approaches That Work In Rural Development

Beyond Prince and Merchant: Citizen Participation and the Rise of Civil Society

Please Forward: The Life of Liza Tod

Dare Me! The Life and Work of Gerald Glaskin

THE BOATMAN

AN INDIAN LOVE STORY

JOHN BURBIDGE

transit lounge

MELBOURNE, AUSTRALIA
www.transitlounge.com.au

Copyright © John Burbidge 2014

Published 2015 by Transit Lounge Publishing
First published in a different version by Yoda Press, New Delhi 2014

All rights reserved. This book is copyright. Apart from any fair dealing for the purpose of private study, research, criticism or review, as permitted under the Copyright Act, no part may be reproduced by any process without written permission. Inquiries should be made to the publisher.

Front cover image: Steve McCurry/Magnum Photos/Snapper Media.
Cover and book design: Peter Lo

ROSE, THE (from "The Rose")
Words and Music by AMANDA McBROOM © 1977 (Renewed)
WARNER-TAMERLANE PUBLISHING CORP. and
THIRD STORY MUSIC, INC.
All Rights Administered by WARNER-TAMERLANE PUBLISHING CORP. All Rights Reserved.
Used by Permission of ALFRED MUSIC

Printed in Australia by McPherson's Printing

A cataloguing entry for this title is available from the
National Library of Australia: http://catalogue.nla.gov.au

ISBN: 978-1-921924-80-4

MIX
Paper from responsible sources
FSC® C001695

To India,
for enabling me to make the leap
and to Bruce,
who caught me when I did.

It's the heart, afraid of breaking
That never learns to dance
It's the dream, afraid of waking
That never takes a chance
It's the one who won't be taken
Who cannot seem to give
And the soul, afraid of dying
That never learns to live.

— *The Rose*

Bombay was chock-full of hidden surprises that never failed to delight me when I stumbled upon them. From postage-stamp public gardens to funky restaurants tucked away down back alleys, it was a city of a thousand faces. Even if I were to live there several lifetimes, I wouldn't know them all. That a large tract of natural bushland existed in this urban cauldron didn't make sense, except that this particular area was a stone's throw from one of the most fashionable suburbs. No doubt a lot of money had changed hands to make sure this precious buffer zone remained. This evening I was very glad of its existence. Finding a private space in which to act out my fantasies would soon become an all-consuming priority in my life. In this, I shared much in common with many Indians. But they had one other skill I was yet to acquire—finding ways of being sexually active in public places.

After about a kilometer, we approached the lower reaches of the park. There were no signs or benches, only a few rough-hewn paths heading off in different directions into the undergrowth. I dutifully followed my companion who chose one of the less-used tracks. As we trudged up the hillside over knotted roots and mossy gravel, it grew considerably darker under the forest canopy that provided us with a cover for our clandestine activities, but which also made me uneasy. Finally, he pointed to a fallen tree trunk in a little niche just off the path.

'You sure it's OK here?' I asked.

'No problem.'

No problem for whom, I wondered. The only exit I could see was the path we had taken to get there. Above us it took an abrupt turn, so there was no way you could see anyone approaching. I was on edge, but my burgeoning desire took care of that.

He motioned me to sit on the log beside him. A twig snapped up the hill and a crow let out a raucous cry. The thunderous roar of the city had been quelled to a rolling hum where the forest began. It gave me a momentary sense of security, enough for me to reach over towards him, gently lift his T-shirt, and slide my hand around his waist. I stroked his back several times before venturing to his front. He didn't protest, so I decided to up the ante and leaned over to kiss him on the cheek. He pulled away, as if in disgust. Instead, he reached over and unzipped me. I was already fully stoked and ready to fire. I took this as my cue and did the same to him.

Just as we were reaching a mutual crescendo, he turned his head away. I was puzzled. Had I done something to offend him? I was about to ask, when he whispered, 'Someone coming!'

He quickly withdrew his hand and pushed mine away, and zipped up with a swiftness that suggested he had this routine down pat. It was then I heard footsteps a few meters away, accompanied by a rush of Hindi. Before I knew what was happening, two men had turned the corner and were headed straight towards us, while a third mysteriously appeared from the path below, sandwiching us. My companion leaped up and darted down the hillside like a startled rabbit. One of the men went racing after him, while the other two closed in on me.

'Aap yahaan kya karte hain?' snapped the older of the two men.

'I don't speak Hindi.'

'What you do here?'

'My friend and I were taking a walk.'

'Don't lie! I know what you do. Sala kutta!'

With that, he slapped me across the face with the back of his right hand, sending a sharp pain rippling through my body and throwing me off balance. As I tried to regain my footing, the other man grabbed my left hand and tugged at my watch. Instinctively, I tried to pull away but was no match for the two of them. He ripped the watch from my wrist, grazing my skin with its metal band. As I looked down to check if I was bleeding, I noticed my umbrella lying on the ground. While my attacker was distracted admiring his prize, I snatched the umbrella. Years of fencing practice suddenly resurfaced and with a vigor that surprised even me, I lunged at the man and whacked him across the shoulder blades, then spun around and caught the other one with a blow to the head. 'Pagal!' he screamed, convinced I was crazy. Then, turning to his cohort, he commanded 'chalo' and the two of them bounded down the hill, leaving me shaking as I slumped onto the log.

I don't know who those men were—plainclothes cops, goondas or just friends out for a bit of fun. It even crossed my mind this may have been a set-up, but it seemed unlikely. I was angry at having allowed myself to be led into such a dangerous situation and vowed never to do so again. But, as I would come to discover, my proclamations were no match for my proclivities.

A PLACE CALLED HOME

It was a muggy August day in 1980 as I stepped off a Singapore Airlines plane at Bombay's Santa Cruz Airport. On the long flight from London I had become enchanted with MM Kaye's epic, *The Far Pavilions*. I arrived still cocooned in its fantasy world of seductive Indian princesses and gallant officers of the British Raj living a life of passion and intrigue on the Northwest Frontier. How seamlessly I slipped into the mystique of that lost era, rather than facing the harsh reality of the present with its overwhelming challenges of rural poverty and urban blight that I, supposedly, was coming to help alleviate. As I turned page after page, I was overcome by the strange notion that I was embarking on a romantic adventure of my own, not one with all the glory and majesty of the Raj, but tailor-made for me, with my quirks and quandaries. Little did I realize then how prescient this would prove to be.

I also had a hunch that returning to India would be a wholly different experience from the painful struggle it had been during my first assignment there four years earlier. At that time, the international non-governmental organization I worked with had launched a large-scale village development project in the state of Maharashtra that needed an infusion of foreign volunteers to help train and work alongside its rapidly expanding indigenous staff to undergird such an ambitious undertaking.

When I returned to Australia two years later, colleagues had stared in disbelief as I walked into the room where they were meeting. There was an unuttered, collective gasp as they glimpsed the ghost of the person they had known. They knew nothing of the devastating cycles of dysentery and diarrhea I had endured, or the countless nights I'd spent sleeping at grimy bus depots and on rock-hard dung floors. They had never tasted the repetitious meals of chili-laced vegetables and leathery rotis that had been my staple diet. And they had no notion of the embarrassment and shame I had felt when I spent my last rupee to pay off our staff's debt to the village kirana shop. We claimed to be promoting economic self-sufficiency and social self-reliance among India's poverty-stricken villages, while our bare-bones budget couldn't even support our own staff.

My peculiar mix of open-mindedness, youthful vision and ingrained Australian stoicism weren't enough to sustain me through this experience, which ripped away the veneer of innocence and naiveté in which I had cloaked myself and left me doubting my own capacities, as well as those of the organization. When my weight dropped under 55 kilograms and my bank account contained about as many rupees, I requested to be assigned back to Australia, ostensibly to be married and care for my aging mother. The truth was, I just couldn't take it anymore. I promised myself never to return to

India. But when asked to go back two years later, I accepted the assignment, albeit with reservations.

Several things made me change my mind. This time, my work as a fundraiser would be in cities, where I would have access to a wide range of food and quality medical services, as well as a permanent residence in Bombay instead of an ever-changing string of village abodes. I had also accumulated a modest cash reserve, should our corporate finances not keep up with demand. And traveling to many countries had taught me to give places a second chance, since first impressions are not always accurate.

Such things were merely a safety net, and a tenuous one at that, but they bolstered my spirits. What's more, I was no longer the novice I had been. I could speak a smattering of Hindi and Marathi, could read a little Devanagari script, and knew enough local places and menu items to dispense advice to new arrivals. If India was not yet my ally, it was not my enemy either. But not even in my wildest imaginings could I have foreseen how radically it would change my life over the next four years. I could not have conceived then that I would go on to meet some of the country's premier leaders, sport stars and artists; that I would make friends with people of every strata of society, from office peons to high court judges; and that India's young men would exercise such a powerful attraction over me that my understanding of myself would be forever transformed.

* * *

India defies preparation; it demands submission. I rediscovered this the moment I set foot outside the terminal building and fought my way through hordes of men to the long line of Fiat taxis that resembled a gigantic black and yellow serpent.

'Sankli Street. Byculla Bridge ke paas,' I announced proudly, getting into the first available taxi.

The driver looked in the rearview mirror as if to check that it was I who had spoken.

'Do sau rupaye,' he demanded.

I didn't know much Hindi, but I did know that 200 rupees for this ride was pure extortion.

'Do sau rupaye nahi. Pachas rupaye.'

The driver promptly switched off his engine to communicate his disgust at my insulting offer. I wondered what he would have done had I offered the official rate of 35 rupees. He then launched into a passionate monologue in Hindi and broken English. I glanced out the window in the vain hope of attracting the attention of the duty officer, but he was nowhere to be seen. I decided to offer 100 rupees and trust my luck.

He muttered under his breath, turned on the ignition, and tore away from the curb, smashing my head against the car door.

Leaving me to nurse my wounds, he turned up his speaker full blast to the thumping beat of a Bollywood dance number; then gently touched the head of Lakshmi, the goddess of wealth, whose angelic presence radiated from an icon at the center of the dashboard.

As he weaved the taxi in and out of smoke-belching traffic, I remembered why I had sworn never to drive in India. In an odd mix of daredevilry and patience, the driver seemed quite calm as he came within a hair's breadth of grossly overloaded trucks and double-decker buses and buffeted his way past slower vehicles, tooting his horn at the last possible moment when changing lanes. The closer we came to our destination, the thicker was the traffic and the slower he drove. As we neared Byculla, familiar sights flashed by—the restaurant where I'd eaten my first meal in India, the market with its stench of rotting fruit and vegetables next to the fire station, and the concrete flyover, festooned with a sea of plastic sheeting on the makeshift dwellings that had sprouted at its base since my last visit.

As we turned sharply into Sankli Street, I leaned over to the driver and pointed to the open gateway on our left.

'Idhar, idhar,' I said, just in time for him to swerve into the driveway and slam his foot on the brake.

I looked up at the second-floor balcony, hoping against hope that one of our Indian staff had noticed my arrival and would float down to assist me like a guardian angel. Since this didn't appear imminent, I decided to get out but was prevented from doing so.

'Driver sahib, door handle nahi.'

The driver turned and handed me the missing part.

'You put it on,' he commanded.

After much fiddling, I managed to attach it and open the door. While I went to the trunk and extracted my case, he stood there, arms akimbo, fixing me with an insistent stare. My moment of reckoning had come, but I resented his pressure tactics, so I took my time opening my wallet, rifling through a wad of notes and counting 50 rupees.

'Sala!' he snarled, following it up with a flood of words I could not understand but whose meaning was patently clear.

Since he had the upper hand, I began to rethink my position. Just as I was about to concede defeat and delve back into my wallet, a young Indian in a navy blue safari suit came strolling through the gate. He was short and slim, with greased-down hair and eyes that sparkled like gemstones. I remembered him well from my previous assignment. I waved and he waved back.

'Namaskar John sahib. Good to see you again. What seems to be the problem?'

Before I could respond, the driver interjected with a torrent of words. Manoj appeared unfazed, so I let the two of them carry on. Then he turned to me.

'He says you promised to pay him 100 rupees.'

I told him the story. The driver butted in, ignoring me while he continued to harangue Manoj. Finally, when Manoj suggested I pay 75 rupees, I didn't hesitate. I had learned to respect his advice on more than one occasion and now felt bad that I'd drawn him into this affair. The driver grabbed the extra 25 rupees, spat on the ground, and made a hasty exit.

Manoj offered to carry my case upstairs but I adamantly refused. I was already indebted to him for rescuing me from a debacle of my own making and had no desire to impose on him again. Besides, I didn't want to give the impression that he and I were anything but equals.

While stuffing my wallet back into my shoulder bag, I glanced up at the arched façade of the three-story building before me, and was overcome by an inexplicable feeling that I had come home. And what an odd place to call home! Close to Mother Teresa's Home for the Destitute and Dying and opposite the local offices of the Bombay Municipal

Corporation, this imposing church served both Marathi-and Kannada-speaking congregations in a culturally diverse part of the city. Within five minutes' walk were a mosque, a Hindu temple, and a synagogue. Set back from the street in a spacious compound, the building was protected from the passing flood of human, animal and vehicular traffic by a high iron fence. Of two sets of forbidding gates, one was permanently locked.

As Manoj and I trudged up the stone staircase, he filled me in on recent developments.

'Henry arrived two days ago. Salima is expected tomorrow and the others should be here by the weekend. Henry wants us to meet right away. Says we have no time to lose.'

The front door was open, so we walked straight through. I was glad to put down my case, loaded with supplies that foreigners were more or less expected to bring from abroad—cheese and chocolates always high on the list. As I entered the main meeting room, heads turned in my direction and people came over to shake my hand, among them two Australians. 'G'day' and 'mate' accompanied the handshakes and backslaps. Hugging was something Americans did on occasions like this, but not Australians, and definitely not Indians. For them, cultural etiquette forbade anything more than a polite namaste or a limp handshake. Bodily contact was reserved strictly for private occasions.

I had never enjoyed being the center of attention but at this point I welcomed the warm reception. The broad smiles with which many of my Indian coworkers greeted me reassured me about my decision to return. They were the most important reason I was here. I had come to share with them my expertise in fundraising and public relations, to support the organization's work in villages. Their trust and respect meant a great deal to me and I had worked hard to earn it. They had especially appreciated my attempt to acquire some facility in local languages during my first stint in India.

But the one person I had expected to see was not in the room. Just as I was about to retrieve my case from the hallway, Henry strode in from the front office, notebook under arm. He was probably no more than five years older than me but his commanding manner left no doubt that he was in charge. Tall and thickset, he had pale, mottled skin and a balding head. The excess talcum powder splattered on his safari suit spoke of his constant battle with Bombay's oppressive climate. He was responsible for a considerable part of our global fundraising budget and took his charge seriously, but his brooding manner and propensity to launch into lectures did not endear him to his coworkers. I had met him a few years earlier, but had never dealt with him at close quarters or on a regular basis. That, as it turned out, was about to change.

As he approached me, Henry extended his hand.

'So you made it OK,' he said.

'Yes fine, thanks. The hardest part was getting here from the airport, as usual.'

A slight smile came over his round face.

'I'm hoping the others will be here by tomorrow or the day after,' he said. 'Either way, we should meet Friday morning. We've got quite a job ahead of us.'

'By the way,' he added. 'You and I and two others are sharing the back room. Yours is the spare upper bunk.'

Given the limited options at our living quarters, this came as good news. The back room was prized space, with its solid wooden door and attached Asian toilet. It also provided access to the rear staircase which, when the metal gate wasn't locked at night, offered an alternative to the more public front door. This I would come to appreciate, the longer I stayed in Bombay.

Since acquiring the premises a few years earlier, our staff had transformed a comfortable, single-family residence into a living and working space for about 30 people, much of it divided dormitory-style by two-meter-high plywood walls that left a gap below the ceiling. These ensured enough visual but no aural privacy. Loose cloth curtains substituted for doors. We lived like the majority of Indians, for whom privacy was an alien concept and a luxury only the rich could afford. Operating in such a confined space called for major adjustments for those of us who were new to India but for our local staff it wasn't an issue; it was just like being a part of a large, extended family living under the same roof.

While traveling from village to village during my last assignment, I had come to regard the Bombay quarters as palatial. Compared to our makeshift living conditions, they were indeed. I had resented the fact that it possessed a refrigerator to supply cold water, that everyone had his or her own bed, that the residents could just pop out and buy a bar of Cadbury's chocolate or a packet of Britannia biscuits whenever they felt like it. Now that I had come to live here, however, my whole attitude towards the place began to change.

After we had exchanged greetings, swapped news and gossip, and I had shared treats, the hubbub died down and people resumed their routines. I had only a day or two to myself and so decided to make the most of that time. After depositing my suitcase in the back room and hanging my shirts and trousers in the remaining space on the clothes rack, I stuffed a few rupees in my pocket and headed down the back stairs and out onto Sankli Street.

Passing through the gate, I glanced down and recognized Charlie on the pavement. There was something deeply comforting yet horribly disturbing about him. Missing an ear, part of his nose, and the fingers of one hand, Charlie was our resident leper. Like a sentry at his post, he knew the importance of location. His three possessions were a straw mat, a worn-out, grey woolen blanket, and a metal bowl that doubled as an eating utensil and his main tool of trade. I watched him fold the blanket using his knees, arm stubs and head. He was said to be a 'good earning' beggar who belonged to a union, in contrast to the tormented souls commonly seen on the streets of Bombay, who are controlled by a hierarchy of thugs. Day in and day out, fine weather or foul, Charlie was there. Around festivals, he would receive new clothes and during the monsoon someone would move him and his belongings to higher ground.

'Namaste, Charlie bhai. Kaisa hai?' I greeted him. I wasn't sure he would recognize me after two years, but I should have known better. I don't know how long he had been watching people pass through that gate, but he seemed to have developed a computer-like memory for faces and names, especially of the legion of foreigners who had come and gone over the years.

As our gazes met, Charlie's eyes lit up and a broad grin stretched across his gnarled face. He waved his stump of an arm in an earnest gesture of welcome. Way down inside me something melted. A connection had been made that I couldn't explain. It felt good, terribly good.

'Theek hai,' he replied, rolling his head from side to side in classic Indian fashion. Like most unschooled foreigners, I had been puzzled by the right-left-right head roll when I first ran into it. Was it a yes, a no, or something in between? I gradually came to appreciate its assuring affirmation, albeit couched in a kind of muted ambivalence. But there was nothing ambivalent about Charlie. His radiating presence made me feel that traveling more than half way around the world to get here was worth every centimeter.

'Aaj achha hai?'

'Bahut achha,' he replied affirmatively.

Most of my exchanges with Charlie were brief, reflecting more my poor language skills than his conversational ability. But it wasn't the length of our dialogues or their limited content that mattered. What was important was the fact that two human beings from such disparate and unrelated worlds could still acknowledge one another. In a country where social intercourse is so rigidly governed by ironclad traditions, this felt like a radical act.

If Charlie occupied the front lines, Parvati assumed the rear guard. I soon discovered that she would appear every morning at our back door to keep an eagle eye on our garbage bins. With wrinkles carved like ancient ravines into her folded skin and a stooped back brought on by years of relentless physical labor, she had aged way beyond her years. What was her story, I wondered. Was she a widow cast out by her family? Had she been forced to leave her village because of a scandal? Was she related to one of the church members? I'd watch her climb the three flights of steps, her frayed green sari tucked up between her spindly legs, to make sure she had the first pickings of the treasures we so mindlessly threw away. As she descended with overflowing bins poised uneasily on her shoulder, I feared that she would collapse under their weight. Step by step, she would haul first one, then the other bin, down to a concrete enclosure at the rear of the compound and meticulously sort through their contents.

The more I watched her doing this, the more I marveled at Parvati. While my heart longed to relieve her of her burdensome existence, my head taunted me with other thoughts. Long before it had become the standard practice it is today, Parvati taught me the value of recycling and reusing. This was underscored for me several months later when I went to the peanut-wallah three doors down and bought several hundred grams of nuts. As I unwrapped the package, I was shocked to find our funding team's tally sheet for the previous month's donations. At first I felt horrified at how thoughtlessly we were sharing our private business with outsiders, but soon realized that thanks to Parvati several people were benefiting from our waste.

On this particular morning, she had already come and gone and I bid Charlie farewell and proceeded down Sankli Street. My first stop was Shah's pharmacy, adjacent to our compound. 'Pharmacy' was somewhat deceptive, considering the limitless range of goods and services offered by this father-and-sons business, which had been operating in the same three-by-ten meter space since 1933. Shah's great sales pitch was 'if we don't have what you want, we can get it by five o'clock.' And they did; how, is a question better not asked. Everything from mosquito coils to videos to taxis to the airport at three in the morning could be had at Shah's. The polished teak and glass cabinets contained an eclectic array of food and household goods that probably hadn't changed much since the shop had first opened. Bottles of Rose's lime juice stood side by side with jars of Epsom salts, children's toys, and mouse traps. I tried to picture the days when British memsahibs would have dropped by to buy a half-kilo of Darjeeling second-flush tea. Gazing at the back of the store, with the rows of burlap bags bursting at the seams with rice, dal and flour, I was struck how more than three centuries of British presence had not changed some things.

Most of my visits to Shah's were for drugs to combat my recurring bouts of dysentery and diarrhea. A quick visit would produce instant medication. Like most street pharmacies in India, Shah's never made the distinction between 'prescription' and 'over-the-counter' drugs. Moreover, the two Shah brothers would always offer a few words of advice on how to take the medication. I never dared ask what pharmaceutical training they had and I wasn't too concerned. Clutching a bottle of tetracycline or metronidazole, I was relieved at not having to go through the hassle and expense of procuring such medicines abroad.

But today I didn't need to buy anything. I chatted with the younger brother, whom I had always found the more approachable of the two. We had barely exchanged greetings when he asked the one question I dreaded.

'So, did you get married?'

I cleared my throat, while trying to come up with a good excuse why I was not.

'No such luck.'

'Luck? What has luck got to do with it?'

In a culture where marriage is a duty, the details of which are primarily the responsibility of parents, my answer came as a complete cop-out.

'And you?' I asked.

'In three months' time. It's all arranged. I'll send you an invitation.'

'Thanks,' I said, with no intention to accept.

As I turned to walk out of the shop, I was overcome by the aroma of fresh chapattis baking on a hot plate. After stepping out, I noticed Saleena, wife of Ali the banana-wallah, cooking their first and probably only meal of the day on their kerosene burner, on the steps of the building that bore the illustrious, if not pretentious, name of Caswanji Mansions. The steps were their home, for which they no doubt paid a sizable fee to the building's owner, not to mention protection money to the local goondas who controlled the accommodation business in this part of town.

Like Charlie, Ali was a permanent fixture in Sankli Street, but his site was even more strategically chosen, where five roads came together to form one of the busiest intersections in Bombay. As I neared the corner, Ali was leaning on the side of his cart that was laden with overripe bananas. Nearly toothless and with a protruding belly that spilled over his waistline, he was clad in a faded green-checkered lungi and a grimy singlet. Originally from Lucknow, Ali was like millions of others who had moved to Bombay to escape the tyranny of being a landless laborer and to try to eke out an existence. By default rather than design, bananas had become his specialty. He didn't boast many worldly possessions but there was one that he was fiercely proud of—an ancient, secondhand Philips radio. I empathized with his attachment to it as my own most valued possession in India was a hand-held shortwave radio. This little instrument had been a lifeline that had kept me from losing touch with reality, especially when I lived in isolated villages.

Ali's grasp of English was about as good as my taxi-driver Hindi, but between the two of us we usually managed to concoct a conversation. The link was cricket. So often in India, my interest in the game opened doors and forged relationships like nothing else. With Ali, it was the common bond that brought us together across vast and otherwise unbridgeable chasms. Be it any international cricket match, Ali would be the first to update me with the latest score in his potpourri of Hindi, Urdu and English.

This morning, I crept up behind him and prepared to ask the price of bananas.

'Kele kitne paise hai?'

When he heard my voice he spun around, and as he realized who it was, his eyes nearly burst out of their sockets. A smile as wide as the Bay of Bengal covered his face as he extended his hand to shake mine.

'Mr. John! You come back to India!' he exclaimed.

'Assalamu alaikum, Ali.'

'Wa alaikum assalam.'

He turned to his cart and cast his eyes over the rather dubious collection of yesterday-looking bananas. Choosing the best one, he placed it firmly in my hands.

'You have it,' he said in the demanding kind of way Indians tend to give a gift.

'Shukriya.'

As I searched my imagination—and vocabulary—for something else to say, Ali jumped in.

'Kitne baje?' he asked, motioning to his wrist.

'Sadhe aath baje,' I reported.

I had hardly finished telling him the time when he took off in another direction.

'Stralia bahut achha team hai.'

'Kabhi kabhi. Bharat ki jai!' I replied, knowing the Indian tendency to belittle their own players when they aren't doing well. This was all it took for Ali to launch into a tirade against Indian cricket that left me floundering, and without a clue about how to rein in this runaway monologue. When he finally paused to catch his breath, I asked him how his business was going.

'Ah, Mr. John. You rich man. Me poor man.'

If he only knew how pathetically poor I was, trying to live on our monthly stipend of 100 rupees. For the average foreigner, even those working in similar fields to my own, this was a laughable amount of spending money. It would barely have bought a three-course meal in a half-decent Bombay restaurant. Ali would never have believed me if I told him, so there was little point trying. To him, anyone who came from abroad must be rich. The fact that I grew up on one side of the Indian Ocean and Ali on the other was one of those things over which neither of us had any control. Like most Indians I met, Ali could never grasp how a country the size of Australia could house so few people. Many would remind me with irksome regularity that India's population grew by one Australia every year.

Ali, Charlie, Parvati, the Shahs and several others formed

a strange collection of souls who acted like a buffer for me between our cloistered community life and the rough-and-tumble of the wider world. For them, I was probably little more than an oddity who inserted himself into their quotidian lives at indeterminate intervals. For me, the longer I stayed in India, the more they became solid pillars in my ever-fluctuating and highly mobile life. A part of me longed to be just like them, to have well-defined daily routines that rotated around the need to earn a living and take care of my basic needs. But, I had chosen a different path.

Like all other adults at our Bombay center, I was assigned a supporting role to our village-based staff who worked all over Maharashtra and a few other parts of India. Our job was to help downtrodden communities devise and carry out economic and social development projects that would allow them to break out of centuries-old deprivation. Unlike many non-governmental organizations, ours did not introduce funds or technical skills in the first instance. We brought a process and a commitment. After selecting a village, we would meet with a large cross-section of residents and conduct a participatory planning process that produced a blueprint for the village's future. We would then send in a team of Indian and foreign staff to live in the village and assist the people to put their plans into action. It was a novel approach for its time, and one fraught with difficulties. There were some successes and many disappointments. Most of those who came from other countries to participate in this ambitious undertaking would leave with the feeling that they were the ones who had undergone 'development,' rather than the communities they had come to serve. But few, if any, would have had quite the same take on this as I did.

TAKING THE PLUNGE

Flora Fountain, the five-way intersection in the heart of Bombay's bustling business district, was one of my favorite parts of the city. From a touched-up postcard, you could almost believe it was Rome or London, with a white-painted statue of the Goddess of Abundance perched elegantly in the midst of swirling traffic and the ceaseless procession of red double-decker buses. Close to Victoria Terminus with its gothic gargoyles and the shady boulevards of the nearby Fort area, it became a centering place for me.

It had now been six months since my return to India. I had learned to navigate its side streets and alleyways just like an old Bombay-wallah. I knew exactly where to find the best fruit juice, the cheapest rice plate, and the most well-stocked, English-language bookstore. The city's once-regal buildings offered glimpses into its imperial past that allowed me to escape momentarily into a bygone age. But on closer examination, their imposing facades gave way to things much less exotic. At ground level, Flora Fountain was home to another of the city's many enterprising groups—the street vendors—purveyors of everything from imported Rothmans cigarettes and 'Rolex' watches to pirated videos and foreign currencies. Their illegal stalls cluttered the pavement, forcing pedestrians to walk on the road instead. Periodically, truckloads of police would descend upon them in a ruthless scourge designed to clean up the city, only to have the vendors defiantly return a few days later.

On most days, I walked briskly to try to avoid salesmen's unrepentant attempts to interest me in their wares, while hoping not to twist my ankle in the gaps lurking between the well-worn stones underfoot. But on this steamy afternoon, I was early for an appointment with one of our regular donors, so I adopted a more leisurely pace. Many hawkers had already taken to the pavement for a nap beside their carts. Meandering along, I came upon a stall with several tables displaying tattered covers of dog-eared paperbacks. I wasn't one to buy anything off the street, but since this seller didn't seem bothered whether I did or not, I decided to take a look at his stock.

Surveying the table, I was intrigued by the variety of material on offer, ranging from Dostoevsky's *The Brothers Karamazov* to Christopher Isherwood's translation of the Bhagavad Gita. As edifying as these may have been, they were much too heavy for my taste. Most of my reading took place on long overnight train rides or tedious bus journeys, during which I had mastered the art of reading standing up, wedged among numerous other bodies, holding on to a seat with one hand and the book in the other. In order to grip my attention, I needed material that was easy to follow and highly action-oriented, so I tended to go for Leon Uris, Robert Ludlum or

James Clavell novels. But there seemed to be no such titles today.

Just as I was about to move on, something at the end of the table caught my eye. It was the February 1981 issue of *Sexology Today*, a thin magazine not much larger than an average paperback. I don't know whether it was the word 'sexology' that did it or the magazine's bright orange cover, but I was intrigued. As I scanned its contents, one article caught my attention. Titled 'A Search for Love: One Man's Experience with Homosexuality,' it had been written by a Californian journalist. I skimmed through the article and decided to buy the magazine. After handing the man behind the table a few rupees, I shoved the copy into my satchel, glanced around to make sure nobody had witnessed my act, and headed towards Fort for my meeting. Throughout the 30 minutes I spent in the director's office, my mind kept wandering from the subject at hand to the magazine in my bag. Straight after the meeting, I made for the first restaurant I could find, ordered chai and samosa, and pulled out the magazine, opening it to the article that had so captured me.

Just below the title was a brief summary: 'The story of one heterosexual man's daring decision to become involved in the gay world in an attempt to resolve his sexual conflicts.' I was hooked. Just this line stirred something deep within me. Without reading the body of the article, I had a strong sense that I had been meant to find it. Nevertheless, I did have several misgivings. The author lived in California and I was in India, worlds apart in every way. He stated that he was in therapy to deal with deep-seated family conflicts, which did not mirror my situation. But what galvanized my attention was his claim that homosexuality was simply a layer of feeling that prevented him from realizing his true heterosexual nature; a tantalizing theory, but not one I was ready to swallow whole.

I had never been consciously aware of my attraction to young men until I came to India. During my first stay a few years before, several strapping village lads had caught my attention with their swarthy hues, tempting smiles, and playful manner. But I had never seen them as potential sexual partners. And I'm sure my own emaciated appearance never offered any incentive to them, should they have had any desire to make an overture. But ever since I had regained my health and returned to India, things had been different. India didn't seem to be the devouring monster it had during that initial visit. I was reveling in city life with its cascading diversity and never-ending change of scene. Everywhere I turned, in buses and trains, offices and cinemas, walking down the street or eating in a restaurant, I kept noticing young men whose beauty and charm begged me to reach out and touch them.

But I wasn't a poofter, a homo, or any of the other degrading epithets I remembered from growing up in 1960s Australia. I was a decent, earnest young man trying to make a positive contribution to the world. How could I possibly be like that? Then again, there was that foreign-languages teacher in high school who would invite me to his home on the pretext of helping him grade papers, then ply me with beer and crayfish. And the Anglican priest I had met in a small country town who insisted on taking me out to dinner at one of Perth's finest restaurants whenever he came to the city. Neither had overtly demanded sexual favors of me and I had had no interest in them, but clearly they had earmarked me as promising potential. In my naiveté—or was it denial?—I had dismissed their solicitations as misplaced attempts at friendship. But India was different. This time, I was the one with the yearning to connect with young men. I wanted their friendship and more. This strange urge rising within me was like a swelling tide that I couldn't ignore.

I read and re-read the article. It was as if a light had suddenly illuminated what had been there all along. By my third cup of chai, I had decided to take heed of this message I had so mysteriously received. No more would I feign sexual interest in women to please others. No more would I ignore the intensely strong pull that Indian men exerted on me, pretending it was merely some cross-cultural fascination when I knew it was much more intrinsic. Just as the author had taken the plunge and immersed himself in the gay world to discover who he really was, so would I embark on a determined effort to 'test my gay potential.'

But how was I to go about this in a country and city where I was an outsider? Unlike America and Australia, India had no gay bars or bathhouses, let alone publications, drop-in centers or support groups. If there were gay men in India, I didn't have a clue where to find them. Only later would I discover that I was surrounded by them almost everywhere I went—at least by men who had sex with other men, most of whom would never call themselves gay, and with whom I had little desire to associate. But there was also a percentage of young men who truly were attracted to their own sex at the core of their being. They came from every caste, religion, linguistic group and economic class. In the next two years, I would come to know members of virtually all such groups.

Just then, however, my big question was where to start looking.

My first feeble attempt was not encouraging. Before I boarded the No. 7 bus to go home, I bought a copy of the evening English-language paper, as I often did, usually just for the crossword. On this occasion, though, I found myself perusing the classifieds section at the back. As I scanned the columns, my eye honed in on a brief ad hedged in a corner: 'Broad-minded young man wishes to meet others similarly inclined.' And a phone number. What on earth did 'broad-minded' mean? Was it a euphemism for kinky sex? Was he gay or straight? What was his agenda?

Two weeks later, I bought another copy of the paper and this time went straight to the classifieds. The ad was still there. I couldn't resist it any longer. I found a public phone in a nearby restaurant and dialed the number. After several rings, a heavy male voice came on the line.

'Yes?'

'Is this 372958?' I inquired.

'Yes.'

'Did you place an ad in the evening paper?'

'Yes.'

I hesitated for a few seconds, trying to compose my next sentence. I didn't want to preempt his answers but I desperately wanted to know what he had in mind.

'You said you are broad-minded.'

'I'm so broad-minded it hurts when I think.'

Since this conversation was going nowhere fast, I decided to cut to the chase.

'So, what are you interested in, sex-wise?'

There, I'd said it! He had to commit himself now.

'Almost everything,' he replied.

'With men and women?'

'Why not?'

I was about to slam down the phone, but something told me to give it one last chance.

'Would you like to meet?' I ventured.

'Would you?'

I wanted to say 'Hell no' but couldn't bring myself to. Instead, I found myself muttering a pathetic 'yes.'

'Okay. When and where?'

I gave him the name of the restaurant I was in and suggested that we meet in two days, at the same time. He agreed. As I put down the receiver, I noticed the tension in my hand. I had no intention of showing up for the meeting, and suspect he didn't either. If this was what it would take to meet someone, I was not sure I even wanted to try. I needed a completely different approach.

* * *

It was quite improbable how I stumbled upon it. One Sunday after lunch, I was sitting on our front porch looking down at the teeming pageant on the street below. Hawkers in shabby rags pulled overloaded carts many times their body weight; paan-chewing clerks with pressed shirts overhanging their narrow trousers went in and out of the municipal building opposite; young women working at the Mother Teresa Home ambled along in their impeccably clean blue and white saris. I'd seen this spectacle hundreds of times but it never failed to absorb me.

Without my noticing, Rakesh entered the porch and plunked himself down on the wicker chair beside me. Thin, gawky and with a mustache much in need of trimming, he was noticeably different from most of his Indian colleagues. Unlike them, he had grown up in a city that had taught him things about life that his village counterparts would only learn by hearsay or from Bollywood movies.

'So what are you up to today?' he asked.

'Nothing much,' I replied. 'I just need to get out of here for a while. Tell me Rakesh, where's all the action in this city?'

Assuming that I was probing for places to pick up women, he proceeded to give me an impressive list that went far beyond the infamous 'ladies in cages' in nearby Kamathipura Lane. Then, quite offhandedly, he added, 'But be careful if you go down to Chowpatty Beach. That's the San Francisco of Bombay.'

I nearly fell off my chair, while trying to maintain a ho-hum façade. His last sentence sent me reeling back to the article in *Sexology Today*. Like a piece of dialogue artfully placed in a movie script, these six words catapulted me into a whole new universe. They were the missing pieces of the puzzle, the next precious clue in the game I had decided to play. For once I didn't mull over the pros and cons of what I should or should not do, but took the unusual step of letting instinct direct me. After indulging in a little more idle gossip, I excused myself, changed into my light blue pants and striped cotton shirt, and headed out the door before my left brain had a chance to kick into caution mode.

Most Bombayites seem to go to Chowpatty Beach to escape from something—the relentless routines of home and work, the prying eyes and ceaseless demands of family, or the deafening cacophony of taxi horns, bicycle bells and screeching brakes that penetrate every corner of this sprawling octopus of a city. In my case, the highly regulated, cheek-by-jowl communal life in the fishbowl we called a staff residence was reason enough. But it was not only that I was running away from something that led me down to Chowpatty Beach that warm April afternoon more than 30 years ago. It was as though I was being called there by a voice deep inside me that had been struggling most of my life to make itself heard. For some unfathomable reason, I decided this once to listen to it.

The 20-minute bus ride to Chowpatty seemed to take hours that day. The sea of people, vehicles and gray-faced buildings became a blur as the double-decker bus lurched from stop to stop before finally arriving at the beach. My stomach writhed, not from the spicy aloo gobi I had eaten for lunch but from the heightened sense of anticipation building up within me. As the bus slowed down, I prepared to leap from the back door, a maneuver I had perfected since Bombay buses rarely come to a complete halt. My feet hadn't touched the ground when a sharp double twang rang out, as the conductor yanked on the cord to signal the driver to move off.

All at once I was in a starkly different world. There was still noise but it was a more modulated, lighthearted noise, interspersed with the pleading voices of children begging their parents to buy them balloons or let them have pony rides. The pavement was still flooded with people but they were strolling and chatting, not feverishly strutting to and fro. A potpourri of smells still enveloped me but not the same nauseating odors of urine and rotting garbage I'd left behind in the city's snaking streets and byzantine bazaars.

I looked around to survey the scene and get my bearings. The alluring whiff of peanuts roasting and kebabs grilling over glowing charcoals competed for my attention with pau bhajis and bhel puris sizzling in what looked like last week's oil. Normally, I stuck to my rule of not eating street food in India. But today was different. I felt ready to step over these lines that I had carefully drawn to protect myself from the vicissitudes of life. I turned to the peanut-wallah and ordered a hundred grams, which he masterfully scooped up and slipped into a newspaper cone.

As I nibbled on the warm nuts, I called on one of my basic principles when in a new place—thoroughly scope out the situation then hone in on aspects of greatest interest. Observe details, take mental notes, and decide on a course of action. I headed down the promenade in the direction of Nariman Point at the other end of the beach where the Air India building and the Oberoi Towers hotel proclaimed another India, so different from the one I had known while working in villages. As I strolled along, I noticed I wasn't the only foreigner enjoying this seafront promenade. But it wasn't the fair-skinned firangis who caught my eye; it was young Indian men with their lithesome build, beckoning manner and natural beauty. Did they know how attractive they were?

I must have been quite preoccupied with these thoughts because when I paused to check my progress, I was amazed how far I had come. I was beginning to feel a little weary, so when a family vacated a bench, I moved right in on it. Such luxuries seldom remain unclaimed for long in India. No sooner had I sat down than another young man materialized beside me. He was probably in his mid-thirties, a little portly, and with a yellowing shirt hanging over his cuffless trousers. I was pretending to ignore him as I finished the last of my peanuts, when he asked, 'Excuse me, do you have the time?'

I had often been asked this question while working in villages where people laboring in fields never wore watches. Watches, like pens, seemed to exert a curious attraction on Indians as some kind of prized status symbol, quite apart from their monetary value. But this was a different question from the one villagers plied me with, not merely because it was articulated in precise English, but, as I would later discover, for a wholly different purpose.

'It's about 4.30,' I replied.

'Accha. You are from abroad, isn't it?'

Fearing that I was about to be subjected to the usual interrogation Indians routinely inflict on foreigners, I made an effort to get up and leave.

'That's right,' I said, hoping he'd get the hint.

'You stay in hotel?'

'No, I live here…with friends.'

I decided to add the last two words in the hope that he would lose interest, but he was not to be deterred.

'You want anything? Hashish, girls, money change…'

'No thanks,' I said, and turned away. Something about him warned me not to reveal my hidden agenda. I headed back to Chowpatty. By the time I reached the beach, three more men had asked me the time. Strange, I thought, that there should be such a strong interest in the time of day on a Sunday afternoon, when many people were off work.

As I ambled along, I noticed several young men walking hand in hand, some with one hand draped around another's shoulder or waist. This sight had jolted me when I first encountered it in India, though I soon realized that it was not uncommon. In Australia, such behavior would have meant only one thing and could have had serious repercussions in the wrong place at the wrong time. But in India and much of South Asia and the Arab world, it would not raise an eyebrow. Young men felt free to express their friendship and affection for one another in such ways. Sexual interest was not implied, although it may not have been out of the question. How I wished I had been able to experience the same while growing up. It made me want to scream out, 'Don't you know how lucky you are, to be able to do this?'

When I reached Chowpatty Beach, the sun had lowered itself over the horizon. The last straggling threads of daylight were making their exit as the evening star appeared low in the western sky. Cool air wafted in from the Arabian Sea as vendors lit their kerosene lamps. I made my way down to the beach that stretched fifty meters to where small waves idly lapped the shore. It was such a contrast to the blazing white, sandy beaches I'd grown up with. This sand was a graying beige and as full of litter as people. No one swam in the water and no one displayed their near-naked bodies while sunbathing on the beach. People drifted up and down, coagulating into small groups around jugglers, acrobats or fire-eaters, but paid no attention to the water that barricaded them into their overgrown metropolis. It was as though this city had turned its back upon the sea and defiantly faced inland.

By this time of day, the throngs at Chowpatty were winding their way home. The circus of entertainers was thinning out as families with children dwindled and the evening crowd began to take over. Within a short time, mangy monkeys and scrawny bears were replaced by another species. Their repetitive cry of 'maalish, maalish' pierced the silence like the first crows early in the morning. They were men, some old, some young, most a dark chocolate brown and rather emaciated. I later learned that many of them came from northern India, from cities like Kanpur, Patna and Allahabad.

I sat on the sand and observed them for a while as they walked up and down with thin cotton towels draped over their shoulders and small bags clutched under their arms. It soon dawned on me that I had just met another of India's service professions—public masseurs. One or two looked quite attractive but I was not about to let them know, since it was sure to influence any economic arrangement we might enter into. I ignored the first few who approached me, feigning disinterest, but intently observing their routine. They would sidle up to a potential customer, start talking with him, then take off together to another part of the beach. This made me even more curious. Finally, I couldn't stand it any longer. When a trim young man with a butter-melting smile approached me, I wasn't able to resist.

'Maalish, sahib? Maalish first-class sahib. Full maalish. Only 50 rupees.'

I wasn't about to spend half my month's stipend there and then, so I bargained with him until I'd whittled him down to 25 rupees. He scowled, then tried his guilt tactic.

'You foreigner. Why you not pay 50 rupees? I give pukka maalish.'

I knew it was useless to argue. Of course all foreigners could easily spare 50 rupees for a cheap body rub. If he had the slightest inkling about my financial condition, he probably wouldn't have even bothered with me. We haggled a bit longer until I pulled out 30 rupees from my pocket and waved them in front of him. He relented and indicated for me to follow him to the darker end of the beach, away from the crowd and intrusive streetlights.

I tramped along nervously, wondering what was in store. Once he found a quiet spot, he laid out his towel and indicated for me to lie down. As he did so, he glanced up and down along the beach to see if anyone was approaching.

'Any problem?' I asked.

'Plice.'

'What about police?' I asked.

'No good. Don't like maalish-wallah. Take money, beat up maalish-wallah.'

I had no doubt that he was telling the truth and no desire to deal with local law enforcement. Apart from the troubling stories I'd heard about the irregular methods of the Bombay police, I was worried that my status as a volunteer with an international organization, if not the organization itself, might be jeopardized should I fall foul of them. What's more, unlike most foreigners, I didn't have the means to bribe my way out of awkward situations.

But this night I wasn't about to let such considerations deter me, as I watched my masseur lay out his tools of trade on the sand. He asked me to take off my trousers so he could massage my legs. I could feel myself trembling. I'd never taken such a risk before. Should I go through with this? Why didn't I quit while I had the chance? Voices of caution were clamoring for my attention, but I resolutely ignored them. I undid the hook on the flap around my waist, unzipped, and pulled off my trousers.

The masseur must have been no more than 18 but he acted with the aplomb of a man much older, as he selected a couple of bottles from his kit, shook them several times, and rubbed their aromatic contents on his hands. For the first time, I noticed his fingers, long and sinewy but as delicate as those of a concert pianist. I wondered how many bodies these fingers had touched. I came from a family firmly entrenched in a tradition where touch between two people, particularly two males, rarely happened. Generations of solid British working-class stock on both sides had made sure of that. But right now, I yearned for his fingers to touch me, as the mesmerizing scent of sandalwood and jasmine worked its magic.

The moment he laid his hand upon my thigh I knew that history was being rewritten. It was as though the heavens opened and blessings showered down upon me. Ripples of pleasure shot up like an electric current through my abdomen to my chest and arms and back down again. Thoughts came and went so fast I couldn't disentangle one from the other. They soon disappeared altogether in a confused haze, subsiding into the most satisfying sensation I had ever experienced. As he gently worked his hands up and down my leg, I could feel my stomach muscles gradually relax. I glanced up and saw a mass of stars, something I had never noticed all the time I had been in Bombay. Had they come out this night just for me?

He worked for several minutes, first on one leg then the other, all the time casting glances to his left and right. The anxiety that had earlier infected me was soon replaced by a sublime sense of well-being that suffused every cell in my body. Don't stop, I said in my head, please don't stop. I didn't want to talk, but just lie back and let him use his supple hands however he would.

I happened to look up and caught his eye. He looked back at me and glanced down at my underwear, which by now had begun to assume an enlarged shape. He winked. I glanced at his crotch and winked back. He looked furtively up and down the beach one more time. Then, without further ado, he moved closer to me, pulled back his kurta, and undid the string of his pajama pants. Clearly, this was intended to be a mutually pleasurable experience.

I was terrified, yet surging with desire. Never had I been in such a compromising situation with another young man. I had waited more than 30 years for this moment and I was not going to let it pass. All those missed opportunities throughout high school and university where timidity and good manners had held me back were about to be redeemed. All those horny scribbles on toilet walls that belonged to another world began to taunt me mercilessly. All those fleeting glances through bus windows, in railway station queues, even in staff meetings, took on a whole different meaning. I looked him in the eyes once more, and he stared straight back at me as if to say, 'Well, what are you waiting for?'

I reached out and touched him. He closed his eyes and smiled, and something deep inside me pulverized into a thousand little pieces.

* * *

My encounter with the maalish-wallah left me dangling over an abyss of fear and fascination. It revealed a part of me I didn't know had existed. It was as though I had just never pressed the right button, asked the right question, worn the correct glasses. I felt alive and confident, exhilarated and energized. And now I wanted more, lots more. It was like my first ride on a roller coaster. The decision to get on was agonizingly difficult and the journey petrifying, but as soon as the ride came to a halt and I stepped out onto the platform, all I wanted was to get back on and do it over and over again. It was as though a voice were calling to me, 'You've done it. You've finally done it! Don't turn back now. Keep going. You won't regret it.'

The last thing I wanted at that moment was to return home. The thought of facing colleagues, making polite conversation, and lying about where I'd been and what I'd been doing appalled me. I decided to linger a while and try to make sense of what had just happened to me. My rational mind was scrambling to comprehend an experience that had been pure, unmitigated emotion. It wasn't used to dealing with such anomalies; no box existed to which it could consign such outrageous behavior. I moseyed along the beach and plopped down on the sand. As I cast around my eyes, I noticed even more maalish-wallahs than I had earlier. They were doing their endless rounds looking for likely customers, a few more rupees to make tomorrow a little more livable. Around 11 pm, when the crowds had thinned to a trickle, I reluctantly stood and made my way to the nearest bus stop. When a bus eventually arrived, I leaped aboard. The few passengers paid scant attention to me, and I to them. I was so lost in thought, I almost missed my stop.

As I entered the gate, I looked up and found the residence

in total darkness. The back gate would be padlocked, so I had no choice but to trudge up the three flights of stairs and ring the door bell. Several minutes passed and nothing happened. I pressed again. Then, after another minute or two, footsteps came shuffling down the hallway. I took a deep breath. The door opened slowly to reveal Sushila in a disheveled sari.

'Sorry I'm so late,' I blurted, knowing she'd probably opened the door several times already this night. Opening the front door late at night was no one's particular responsibility. Whoever couldn't stand the bell ringing any longer usually ended up doing it. It was a thankless and unceasing task, one of those things everyone came to accept as part of living in this building, along with power outages, bedbugs, and cockroaches.

Sushila said nothing, but looked furtively in my direction before scuttling back to her room. I wondered what that glance had told her. I felt like I was carrying a huge placard announcing to the world the incredible experience I had just had. I slunk down the hallway and into the back room. As I entered, the sound of heavy breathing filled the room. I undressed and pulled myself up to my top bunk, trying hard to mask the noise of straining wire beneath the mattress. One of my roommates turned over and a mosquito buzzed in my left ear. I lay perfectly still, staring at the white paint curling off the moonlit ceiling. My mind was racing a mile a minute, leapfrogging from thought to thought, regurgitating everything that had happened to me in the last six hours. The first hint of daylight seeped through the curtained windows before I finally managed to fall asleep.

A TASTE FOR MORE

Part of what made our organization unique was its internal life. Our staff lived as a community, in both villages and cities, sharing meals, housework, living space, and most of our time. We'd spend endless hours together, to study a book, wrestle with our finances, or plan for the coming week. We would rise early, greet the day with a ritual that included readings from the likes of Gandhi and Tagore, and meet for an hour before breakfast. The meetings would begin with songs from our community songbook, an eclectic mix of Indian and Western tunes, many of whose original words we had modified to reflect the mission and values of the organization. I'm sure our neighbors didn't cherish being woken at six in the morning to a rousing rendition of 'All Life is Open' to 'Guantanamera,' or 'Raghupati Raghava Raja Ram.' But our strange ways seemed to blend in with the plethora of other activities that took place in and around our building, be it a wedding in the church below or a morcha picketing the city offices opposite. Toleration of competing intrusions in their lives was a quality most Indians seemed to develop early on. In our case, the fact that we possessed the only telephone in the building no doubt contributed to our neighbors' forbearance.

The telephone was a blessing and a curse. It could take years to obtain one, not to mention hefty bribes to telephone company managers and technicians. Once you managed to have one installed, the chances of it working were slim. Crossed lines, inordinate delays for long-distance calls, and frequent breakdowns, especially during the monsoon, made it a vexatious instrument. For our fundraising team in particular, it was a critical tool of trade. We needed it to make appointments, keep in touch with our associates around the world, and coordinate travel across the country. When it was out of order, it stymied our whole operation and emotions sometimes boiled over, especially among our foreign staff. Our Indian colleagues were much more inured to such irritations.

Pam was a case in point. She had only arrived from the US a few months earlier and was having a harder time than most adjusting to India. Although she had a reputation as a successful fundraiser, her tolerance quotient was lower than that of most other team members, especially when things weren't going as planned. One Friday morning, at the end of a particularly frustrating week that she had mostly spent trying to arrange appointments for an upcoming trip, her patience gave out.

'No, not three, two!' she bellowed into the handset. 'Two one seven six five five.'

'Three one seven six five five,' the operator repeated.

'No, no, no! Two, you know, two four six eight. That two. The number after one.'

'Three four six eight. Sorry madam, but that is not a proper number.'

The enunciation of the word 'two' in Indian English demanded a tightening of the lips in order to be understood. Those of us who had been in India for some time usually mastered it but Pam had not yet met the challenge. I was in the kitchen drinking water when I heard the sound of the telephone hitting the wall. The force with which Pam wrenched the phone from its wall socket and sent it hurtling across the room—narrowly missing Manoj in transit—was enough to shame a baseball pitcher. As I returned with a glass of water in my hand, I nearly collided with her as she stormed out of the office and through the front door. 'Goddamn India!' were her parting words.

The telephone also connected us to several of our neighbors in the building, who would sometimes receive calls at our number; only one person also used it to make calls. Raju, the church sexton, lived with his family in a tiny ground floor flat, which he treated like a sentry post to eye comings and goings at the rear of the building. His perpetual grin and obsequious manners turned me off. His constant invitations to tea and sweets smacked of favors yet unasked. He'd appear unannounced in our office, sidle up to the phone, and speak as if no one else was in the room. 'Hallooo. Hallooo,' was his signature opening, in half-singing tone. He would punctuate his speech with repeated accha's and achchcha's and occasional haanji's. His calls were mostly brief but he never offered to pay for them. He acted as though it was his inalienable right to use the phone.

Another resident of the building with whom we regularly interacted was the mali. No more than 150 centimeters tall with thinning hair, he was a mali in name only; I doubt if he knew the difference between a neem tree and a nimbu tree. His main role seemed to be taking care of the building's water system. Like milk and other basic commodities in the city, water was strictly rationed. Supply was restricted to half an hour each morning, during which time we would fill several 55-gallon drums and as many buckets as we could. Most days this occurred between 6 and 6.30 am, also the time for our morning gathering. To ensure the drums were filling, the mali would visit both our bathrooms, which were at opposite ends of our meeting room. He would amble across the room, seemingly oblivious to the 30-odd souls seated around the table, and poke his head into the bathrooms. Barefoot and covered only by a thin T-shirt hanging outside his boxer shorts, he was an amusing sight. We became used to his morning apparitions and paid little attention to them, but guests would stare blankly in disbelief.

Our common lifestyle, with its daily and weekly rhythms lent stability to our existence and acted as a buffer to the chaos of the world outside. For those of us traveling constantly throughout India for fundraising, staff training, financial management or other tasks, our Bombay residential office was a safe and secure haven to return to. It was light years removed from the luxury apartments that many expatriates came home to each evening in their chauffeur-driven cars. It did not even resemble the comfortable abode that the clergyman and his four-person family occupied in the very same floor space below us. But it was ours and I treasured it. For the most part. On some days, this very regimented lifestyle made it feel more like a prison than a home. There were times when I couldn't wait to get out.

This was one of those times. I found myself counting the days until the next Sunday afternoon that I would have to myself, when I could head to Chowpatty Beach once again; if for nothing else, then just to confirm if what I thought had happened wasn't a gigantic illusion.

Unfortunately, this would have to wait three weeks as I was sent to Calcutta on a fundraising trip and didn't return until the end of the month. When the day finally arrived, I could scarcely contain my rising anticipation. As soon as we dispersed for the day, I changed clothes and headed for the front door. On my way out, one of my American colleagues hailed me.

'Where are you off to in such a hurry?' he asked.

I resented these interrogations, but living and working in close quarters, they came with the turf. I decided to give him one of my standard replies, slightly enhanced to make it sound more authentic.

'I'm going to visit a friend. His family's invited me to lunch.'

'Shooting the breeze, eh?'

'Yeah, you could call it that,' I replied. 'See you later!'

It dawned on me that I should be more discreet in leaving the house if I wished to protect what minuscule privacy I had. I could have exited via the back stairs instead of the front door, but then I'd have risked running into Raju. I made straight for the bus stop and soon found myself at Chowpatty Beach. It was still early afternoon, so I had time to kill before the maalish-wallahs made their appearance. I decided to follow the same route as before and walked along Marine Drive to the other end of the bay. Night photographs of this part of the city carry the glamorous caption of 'the Queen's necklace,' cleverly disguising the squalor and seediness hidden in the gutters and back streets within spitting distance of the promenade.

I took my time surveying the crowd and kept an eye open for potential contacts, but none were obvious. Since it appeared I was too early, I headed for a local bar and ordered a bottle of Hayward's beer and some papadam. I hardly ever drank a whole bottle of beer, since Indian beer only came in large bottles. When I stood to leave, I felt strangely light-headed and decided to make for the beach where a gentle breeze was blowing. Clouds had rolled in and there was a whiff of rain in the air, which made me glad that I had brought my umbrella. I sat on a stone wall that separated the sand from the pavement. Within minutes, a slight young man wearing a green Adidas T-shirt had deposited himself beside me. He glanced in my direction then away again. A buzzer started going off in my head.

'You visit Bombay?' he asked.

'No, I live here.'

As soon as I'd said it, I began to regret it. To most Indians, living here as a foreigner conjured up images of having your own apartment, endless money, exotic goods, and easy access to travel abroad.

'What work you do?'

'I'm a volunteer in a village development project,' I replied.

He blinked as he tried sifting through what I had said. Obviously, I didn't fit neatly into his preconceived notions of a foreigner. But something told him not to bother about such inconsistencies.

'You like homosex?'

'Homosex!' The word hit me like a whack on the head. I'd never heard it before. Was this Indian English? Should I add it to my growing lexicon of usable words?

'Maybe.'

'You like me?'

'Perhaps.'

'You have place?'

This guy didn't waste any time getting to the point. He was your straight-down-the-middle businessman, a type I later came to know as a 'commercial boy' and of whom I learned to steer clear. But just then my instincts weren't so finely honed. He represented immediate gratification, something I'd rarely succumbed to but now was beginning to be consumed with.

'No, I live with friends. Our place is very crowded. How about you?'

'I live with my auntie and cousin brother. But I know a place we can go.'

'Where?'

'Up there,' he said, pointing to the tree-covered slope on Malabar Hill below the manicured Kamala Nehru Park and the Hanging Gardens.

'It's safe?'

'No problem. There are private places.'

All the while we chatted, I found myself admiring his youthful looks and slender physique, not to mention his self-assured manner. As we sat there, I began mentally undressing him, something I'd never done before with anyone. My imagination kicked into high gear and a growing desire began blotting out the alert messages being sent out by the more cautious part of my mind. I glanced at my watch. It was approaching 5 pm. The light was dimming but it would be some time before darkness moved in and took over.

'OK. Show me the way.'

He jumped up and began striding towards the road, so I had to move swiftly to keep up. He crossed the six lanes with great ease, slipping in between cars and motorcycles like a fish darting through water. He waited for me to catch up and then proceeded at a fair pace, as though he was as anxious as I was to begin our tryst. I had my doubts about there being such a place in this non-stop city, where every square meter of land was used many times over for some purpose. But another part of me wanted so much to believe it that I followed him slavishly.

What happened next not only left me physically bruised and minus my precious watch, but it shook me to the core. The pummeling I received at the hands of the men who surprised us in the forest obliterated the euphoria of sexual awakening I had experienced only a few weeks before. My confidence to continue on my quest of sexual exploration had been dealt a massive blow. The risks of having sex with a stranger in a public place now terrified me. But what other options did I have? Was this the price I would have to pay to 'test my gay potential'? How clinically academic that phrase sounded now. Perhaps I should back down before I suffered serious injury or risk to my reputation. As my bus lumbered from stop to stop, my mind darted in different directions. Deep down I knew I couldn't just walk away from this game I was playing with myself. But then I realized it was so much more than a game. It was something fundamental to who I was as a human being, and I had to pursue it. What really scared me was that, in spite of this shattering experience, there was something about it that was not totally distasteful.

* * *

I steered clear from the ill-fated parkland after that, but I wasn't deterred from scouting for safer options. Bombay's city planners had had the foresight to include a large open area in the heart of the city's business district between the two major railway stations, Victoria Terminus and Churchgate. Known as the maidan, the grassed playing field offered welcome relief to office workers during the week and played host to hundreds of overlapping cricket games during the weekend. At night it became a refuge for couples seeking that rarest of commodities in India—a place to escape the gaze of one's neighbor. I soon figured out that it would also provide the same attraction for gay men.

Reconnoitering the maidan began out of intuition and developed into an obsession. I began taking every opportunity that presented itself to explore its precincts, mainly after sunset. I fancied myself as a spy in a John le Carré novel, sussing out the terrain for possible rendezvous points with my handler. These nocturnal forays charged me up in a way that none of my fundraising and public relations work came close to doing. As the urge to keep venturing out grew stronger, so too did my concern about arousing suspicion among my colleagues. Living and working in such close proximity with them, I felt like a permanent blip on their radar screen.

Although most of our evenings were devoted to community activities, some nights were designated personal. I made a point of going out with my colleagues from time to time to maintain relationships with those I regarded as friends and to camouflage my other activities. We usually went to local restaurants that offered refreshing alternatives to our routine sabzi and chapattis. As much as I enjoyed these diversions, even these too became part of my secret life, as I found myself checking out the waiters and fellow diners for desirable men.

While the maidan attracted a variety of evening adventurers, I soon learned that other places in the vicinity were more specifically identified as gay hangouts, most notably the Bandstand, or BS, in local gay parlance. Separated from the maidan by a major road and a traffic roundabout, the Bandstand was a small, cultivated park with an ornate rotunda in the middle. One could imagine a military band playing here on Sunday afternoons to a largely British audience in bygone days. Nowadays, Sunday afternoons were given over to a children's fair with pony rides around the circular path that dominated the park. But from about 8 pm onwards, it would turn into an entirely different place.

Saturday was usually the busiest night of the week, but the makeup of the crowd was completely unpredictable. A variety of men were drawn to the Bandstand—young and not-so-young, Hindu and Muslim, Sikh and Christian, rich and poor, lovers and the unloved, even the odd foreigner. The Indian Navy Men's Hostel down the road was a source of many of its visitors. The crowd ebbed and flowed, occasionally spilling over into a dark laneway behind the park. Some ogled newcomers with a flirtatious eye, while others simply delighted in being in a place where banter could flow freely and they could let down their guard, if only for a few precious hours.

My first visit to the Bandstand coincided with a program I was assigned to conduct with an international bank in Bombay. One of the Institute's legacies from its community development work was a strategic planning process adapted for use in the corporate world. Fees from these courses not only boosted our staff income, but also raised our profile as organizational change consultants among Indian businesses. Companies would usually provide first-class accommodation for our facilitation team, but since our entire faculty resided in Bombay, we agreed to something less expensive, as long as we could have a place to work after hours. I suggested a guesthouse I had heard of, run by a foreign couple and not far from the course location. When we arrived to inspect the place we were not disappointed. Not a speck of dust to be seen, no clashing colors on the walls. Finely crafted teak chests and shiny brass plates gave it an elegance associated with much pricier establishments. But it was the pictures of Jesus with blood dripping from holes in his palms that made me do a double take. In a land where religious icons abound such pictures were not uncommon, but in this case we had stumbled on a particular brand of devotee—the foreign missionary who had never left. They often exhibited a pious morality that made me uncomfortable. I glanced at my colleagues and they at me. Raised eyebrows said it all. We would have to be on our best behavior.

The course proceeded smoothly and at the end of the last day my colleagues decided to return to the staff residence and their families. However, since we had already booked the accommodation for an extra night for any pending work, I volunteered to stay behind. The gesture provided a perfect cover for my personal agenda. The guesthouse, which was on the second floor of a medium-rise apartment block, was a five-minute walk from the Bandstand. It was an appealing combination of factors—free, private accommodation away from the scrutiny of others and close to one of the most well-known places to find gay men in all Bombay. How to connect the two, and come away unscathed, was the challenge.

I finished my work in an hour and a half and proceeded to the Bandstand. While the fringes were lit by streetlights, the innermost reaches were so dark you could barely see a person's face a few centimeters away. Most people were seated on benches along the pathway or standing and chatting in small groups. Before entering the park, I idled up and down the pavement, feigning a nonchalance that suggested I was a tourist out for a stroll. When a bench became vacant, I took it as my cue and sat down on one end of it, leaving the other conspicuously vacant. Several young men paraded themselves in front of me, casting a curious eye in my direction. None of them particularly interested me so I refrained from making a welcoming gesture. My experience in the other park had taught me to err on the side of caution.

Just as I was considering leaving, a tallish young man who had been circling the rotunda like a shark eyeing its prey came and sat next to me. Solidly built, his black-rimmed glasses gave him the air of a college student, an impression reinforced by his excellent English and forthright manner.

'I don't think I've seen you before. Are you new here?'

'New to the Bandstand, not to Bombay.'

'You in business?'

'No, I'm with an international development organization.'

This appeared to satisfy him because he abruptly changed tack.

'You know what goes on in this park?'

'I have a pretty fair idea, this time of night.'

He smiled and edged a little closer to me. I lapped my arm around the back of the seat so it gently fell onto his shoulder. He pulled away immediately.

'Better not do that here,' he whispered.

'Really? I thought it was fairly safe.'

'Not always. You never know when plainclothes cops might show up.'

I shuddered. I found it hard to believe that the police would raid such a public place, but would later see how wrong I was.

'You have a place?' he asked.

'Well, it so happens I do tonight. And it's quite close to here. But we'll need to be very careful. I'm a guest and there's a chowkidar at the door.'

'No problem. I can be discreet. And I can handle chowkidars.'

Discreet. Was this guy an English major, or just your average well-educated Indian? Either way, his professed ability to deal with night watchmen raised him a notch or two in my assessment of him.

'By the way, my name's Graham,' I said.

'I'm Naresh,' he said. 'Shall we go then?'

'Chalo,' I replied.

This encounter was so different from my first ill-fated one at the parkland that I began to feel emboldened as we walked towards the guesthouse, at the same time reminding myself that it wasn't time to celebrate quite yet. There were still a couple of hurdles to clear if this evening was to become all it promised.

The presence of night watchmen in most buildings in India made late-night entries a delicate, if not impossible, affair, although a few rupees or a bottle of cheap liquor could change things significantly. In this instance, the chowkidar had seen me come and go a number of times in the last few days, so he had no reason to be suspicious. It was the presence of my Indian companion that I was worried about. But I decided to trust Naresh's word and let him handle the situation if one were to arise. As we approached the entrance, I began babbling to Naresh to give the impression that we were busily engaged in discussion, in the hope that it would deter the chowkidar from intervening. Thankfully, it worked.

Just one more potential obstacle. I had to take Naresh from the front door of the apartment to my bedroom without being seen. This involved a short walk across an open living room. Praying that the couple who ran the place wouldn't still be up, I rapidly tried to assemble a backup story to explain his presence, just in case.

'Wait here,' I commanded Naresh when we reached the apartment door, as I slid my key in the lock and gently nudged open the door. The lamp-lit sitting room was silent. I waited a few seconds then padded over the Afghan rug as silently as a cat and opened my bedroom door, before retracing my steps to the front door and motioning to Naresh to come in. When we were both safely inside my bedroom, I breathed a sigh of relief, locked the door, and turned on the bedside lamp.

'You mind if we don't have the light on?' he asked.

'Not at all. In fact, it's probably a good idea. And let's

be careful not to make any noise. I don't want to arouse suspicions.'

I leaned over and switched off the lamp. He took off his glasses and we collapsed onto the bed. An hour and a half later, Naresh left as surreptitiously as he had come.

I was ecstatic. I had taken a huge risk and it had paid off. I felt like yelling at the top of my voice, announcing to the world my great achievement, although I dared not utter a word. It would be more than a year before I told anyone about my newly discovered secret. I sprawled on the bed and tried to relive the fleeting moments we had enjoyed together, knowing full well they were already consigned to the annals of history. Turning over, I wallowed in the sheets that retained his musky odor and drops of sweat from our writhing bodies. I could never fathom why foreigners found the odor of Indians repugnant. I couldn't get enough of it. It had a rawness and strength that was as sweet and compelling to me as nectar to a humming bird. I put my fingertips to my nose and inhaled before drifting off into a deep sleep.

***

I saw Naresh only once after that, and most unexpectedly. I was taking the Rajdhani Express to Delhi with an Indian colleague. We had just boarded the train at Bombay Central and I was walking through the carriage next to mine. I stopped dead in my tracks when I saw him. He was lifting a heavy case to an upper rack for an older woman. They were engaged in conversation as I came up behind him.

'Hi Naresh.'

He turned and gasped when he saw me.

'Oh hi,' he replied. 'You going to Delhi too?'

'Yeah, for about 10 days. And you?'

'I'm going with my mummy. We're making plans for my marriage.'

I tried not to look too shocked or disapproving. I knew all about arranged marriages and how few gay men could find a way around them, even if they wished to. I felt sad, for him and for the young woman whose husband he would become. Nine out of 10 gay men I would come to know in India would see no option but to marry, in order to fulfill their obligation to continue the family line and to create offspring to care for their parents in old age. Naresh was the rule, not the exception.

'Maybe we could meet up in Delhi?' I suggested.

'Maybe,' he replied with a distinct ring of 'don't bother' about it.

We exchanged phone numbers. His became one of the dozens that I accrued over the next two years. Even though we didn't speak again, the memory of our precious time together never deserted me.

DIGGING DEEPER

The Bandstand soon became my regular stamping ground. Whenever I had a free evening I would go there to see what new windows I could prise open on my shuttered life. My mounting desire for contact with other young men led me to take ever greater risks. For the first time in my life, I had a clue about what other guys meant when they said a woman 'turned them on.' Only in my case the woman was a man, usually young with brown skin, slight stature and a knee-weakening smile. Within a few months, I had become a regular at the Bandstand. I made countless connections there, some of which developed into lasting friendships, while others disappeared into impenetrable crevices of my memory.

From my travels to other Indian cities, I learned that the Bandstand held an iconic status among gays throughout the country. Never was this more evident than on New Year's Eve. Long before the midnight hour, dozens of men began filling its precincts till it was overflowing. Freshly pressed white kurtas swished side by side with denim jeans. Neatly trimmed mustaches vied with sailors' beards and Sikh turbans. Some came on foot or by bus, others in taxis and chauffeur-driven cars. Rumors spread faster than wildfire before a raging wind. 'Did you hear that Bollywood's favorite pin-up boy was seen cruising by in his imported Cadillac?' 'Can you believe that the guy holding hands with that cute young thing is actually a cop?' Stories bubbled, old acquaintances were renewed, and affection flowed freely. In a country where homosexuality was illegal, social pressures and cultural mores were strongly homophobic, and no public gay establishments existed, the Bandstand on 31 December was like a blazing beacon in an ocean of darkness.

But the high spirits and tender moments were shortlived. The Bandstand was also a preying ground for thieves and thugs, as well as a popular target for police raids. There were frequent reports of money or watches being stolen and of men being bashed in the dark lane at the rear of the park. My early skepticism about these claims was soon eroded, particularly after the night I met Shanti, a tall 25-year-old Gujarati dentist, in a shadowy corner of the maidan. After brief introductions, we retired to a nearby café where he told me his story.

'It was really horrible. I didn't realize what was happening at first. I was sitting alone on a bench at the Bandstand, eyeing the crowd. Out of the blue, two men came and sat on either side of me. One produced a knife and demanded that I empty my pockets. They took my watch and wallet, then raced off. I wanted to scream, but what good would it have done? No one would have noticed or cared. The worst part was that they found my business card. I started getting threatening phone calls demanding money. There was no way I could pay, so I finally went to the police. A fat lot of good that did! They only wanted their cut too. When I refused, they contacted my family and told them the story. I had shamed our family's good name. I thought my father might throw me out of the house and disinherit me. Instead, he demanded I undergo electric shock treatment to cure me of this terrible disease.'

'You didn't give in to his demands, did you?'

'What could I have done? You are a foreigner. You don't understand what it's like to be an only son in a Hindu family. It's okay for you to say I should have refused the treatment. Try stepping into my shoes and see what it's like.'

I didn't know how to respond. Instead, I slipped my right hand under the table and held his left hand.

'I must go now,' he said, catching me off guard. 'Maybe we could meet again some time.'

I made my usual excuses about not having a place of my own but this didn't deter him.

'You have a pen?' he asked.

I produced an old ballpoint and he scribbled down an address on a scrap of paper.

'This is my dental clinic. Come after 8 pm any night except Sunday.'

I folded the paper and slid it in my pocket. For the first time in my life, I couldn't wait to visit a dentist.

* * *

On nights when the Bandstand didn't offer much interest, I would scour the maidan for parts where I was most likely to run into other young men with similar interests. Although some sections were lit by streetlights, others were well secluded from public gaze—not just dark corners or along the stone walls abutting the park, but even the midfield.

I discovered this one Friday night. This was no ordinary Friday night, although to the majority of Indians it would have been. It was Good Friday, celebrated only by the country's tiny Christian minority. But it was a special day for me. Due to an exceptionally heavy workload in the previous couple of months, our staff had decided to take time out. For several days, we were left to our own devices, a rarity in our regimented lifestyle. Because this was a last-minute decision, I had time on my hands I wasn't anticipating. My first thought was how to meet other young men. I flipped through my ever-expanding address book, trying to decide whom to call. But my first challenge was finding a place to stay.

Within five minutes' walk from our staff quarters was a Jesuit-run men's hostel that offered rooms at moderate rates. It also included a dining room for breakfast and snacks. I had learned of its existence from others at the Bandstand and had often passed it by, but had never ventured in. I had reservations about it though. It was so close to home that I might run into colleagues. Also, it was designed primarily for young Catholic men from out of town as a place to stay until they found other accommodation. The first issue I could handle by being doubly alert while entering and leaving the building (although I would later discover how misplaced this confidence was). The second matter proved trickier.

Armed with a small overnight bag, I headed for the hostel. When I reached the registration desk, I noticed that the cost per person diminished as the number of occupants grew.

'Yes?' asked the wiry clerk with double-thick glasses.

'Do you have a room for the next three nights?'

'Which room is it you are wanting?'

'A double room, please. I'm expecting a friend to join me tomorrow.'

I noticed a sign on the counter advising that guests are issued with a pass they must carry with them at all times.

'No doubles. But I have a triple for two nights. After that, I am not knowing.'

'I'll take it.'

'Sixty rupees and sign here,' he said, pushing a gigantic register towards me.

He eyed me like a hawk as I wrote the address of our staff residence in West Bengal.

'You are from Calcutta side, isn't it?'

His gift for stating the obvious impressed me. It was now my turn to watch as he filled out my pass. His elegant longhand flowed from the gold-tipped fountain pen onto the white card. It was only while spelling my name that he stumbled a bit.

'Here is your pass, Mr. Boor-bid-gay,' he said, spitting it out syllable by syllable. 'And what is your friend's good name?'

My mind swung into overdrive, trying to conjure up a common Bengali name, since my imaginary friend would most probably be coming from Calcutta too. I coughed and cleared my throat to buy myself some time.

'Sunderjit Chatterji,' I declared.

As soon as I had said it, it occurred to me that I should have probably given a Christian name rather than a Hindu one. But the clerk didn't seem fazed by it. After noting it down, he slid both passes towards me along with the room key.

'Thank you,' I said.

'No mention.'

I hurried to my third-floor room and unlocked the door. I couldn't believe how spacious it was. I hung my few clothes in the leaning armoire and spread out my writing materials on the desk by the window. It was late morning, so I tried phoning several guys, hoping to arrange an afternoon or evening rendezvous. Two didn't answer and one call resulted in an abortive attempt to communicate with a family servant. Since I couldn't leave a number for any of them to call back, I decided to try again later.

The rest of the day passed pleasantly, as I visited my favorite bookstore, watched *The Great Escape* for the third time, and enjoyed spicy mutton dhansak at a Parsi restaurant. After returning to the hostel early in the evening, I tried phoning again. This time I got through to my dentist friend and we arranged to meet the following day. But I still had no date for the evening. Frustration was beginning to turn to irritation. For once I had a place of my own but no one to share it with. That seemed like nothing short of sacrilege. But I still had one more option. I hopped on a bus and headed for the maidan.

When I reached, the last slivers of daylight were fast disappearing through the fronds of coconut palms that bordered the maidan. I did several rounds of the perimeter but found little activity. Beginning to despair of my luck, I sat down on the grass and scanned the open space. After a few minutes, I heard a noise behind me.

'Skiskiss.'

There it was again, a kind of hissing sound. I looked in the direction it came from and squinted. About 10 meters away from the shadows of the ivy-covered fence emerged a young man. He summoned me with a bent hand. The first time I had come across this gesture in India I had thought I was being shooed away, when in fact it implied the opposite.

I hesitated. Prudence told me to get up and walk a few paces so the streetlight would give me a better view of him. I did and waited to see if he would follow. Within seconds he was alongside me. He didn't appear to be rough trade, but I was not willing to take him back to the hostel. My need for immediate gratification had been simmering all evening and was reaching boiling point. I didn't bother with the usual preliminaries.

'Shall we go and sit in the middle?' I suggested.

'Yes, but down the other end where the light is not so much.'

Was this a genuine attempt to find us more privacy or was he setting me up? Did he have a couple of accomplices lurking over there, ready to fleece a gullible foreigner? I decided to take a chance. We wandered across the maidan and sat down in the center of the field. The grass was slightly damp, so my companion took out a red gamchha and placed it on the ground beneath him, as I'd seen many Indians do on trains and buses. I found this custom quaint at first and silently ridiculed it. But like many things Indian, I gradually warmed to it. It seemed to be a way of claiming public space as one's own, as much as protecting clothing.

I moved my body close to his and bent one leg at the knee, in an effort to screen our activities from curious eyes. At the same time, I searched the field to see if anyone was approaching. Since he was facing me, he could keep a watch on the other side. Satisfied that we were undisturbed, I gently pulled his shirt out of his unbelted trousers and directed my hand towards his crotch. He reached down and unzipped his pants. The invitation was impossible to resist. As I leaned over to grasp him, he did the same to me. Within minutes we had driven each other into a frenzy.

A sharp thwack across my back told me that we were not alone. A stinging pain shot through my body as I jerked my head around to find a khaki-clad policeman leering over me, a wooden lathi gripped in his right hand. He smashed it down onto my companion's shoulders while hurling a tirade of abuse. Red lights flashed in my head and self-preservation kicked in. I jumped up, twisting to dodge another blow from the flailing lathi, and ran. Shouts of 'band karo' didn't deter me. Dredging up my last ounce of energy, I tore across the maidan towards the exit. A sharp whistle blew. I expected a flurry of cops to join the fray. As I belted through the gate into the open street, heads turned and voices rose from the crowd on the pavement. I darted around the corner, sped down the street, and headed for the main road. Gasping for breath, I held out my arm to flag down a taxi.

'Byculla Bridge ke paas. Jaldi, jaldi!' I gushed, before quickly getting in and collapsing in the back seat.

As soon as my back made contact with the vinyl seat, I yelped with pain. It was only then that I realized how bad the wounds were. I was worried that blood might stain my cotton shirt, but tried not to think about it as the taxi sped down Mohammed Ali Road. When we were within a block of the hostel, I asked the driver to stop, slapped a bunch of rupees into his hand, and jumped out. As I entered the hostel and mounted the stairs, the night watchman gave me a cursory look and returned to chewing his paan. I went straight to the bathroom, took off my shirt, and examined my injuries in the mirror. Several welts had formed where the lathi had bruised my skin. I returned to my room, dropped onto the bed, and cried myself to sleep.

The next morning, after a shower and breakfast I felt a little revived, but the pain emanating from my back reminded me of the ugly events of the night before. I sat at the desk, opened an aerogramme, and tried to pen a few words to a friend in New Zealand. I had written to him several months ago, daring for the first time to reveal my newfound sexuality. He was the one person I had decided I could trust. Not only had he known me for many years, he was also a religious brother, who I knew would treat such news with discretion. For weeks I had waited anxiously for a reply, but none came. Then, a few days ago while flicking through my mail, I noticed Jeremy's unmistakable handwriting. I tore open the envelope and held my breath.

With each sentence I read, I uttered a sigh of relief. His words were affirmative and his tone supportive. His caution about taking risks in a strange country with different rules and potential misunderstandings rang true, but in an abstract kind of way. Now I was faced with the embarrassing task of telling him exactly how I had ignored his advice and the price I had had to pay for it. I stared out the window and pondered how to begin. Then I happened to glance above the door. Every room in the hostel probably had one, and I couldn't believe I hadn't noticed it before—a painted effigy of Jesus nailed to the cross. This familiar symbol took on a whole new meaning for me. I picked up my pen and began to write.

I dared not discuss these things with my colleagues and my

Indian gay friends wouldn't have been able to grasp the strange world I inhabited. But thanks to Jeremy, I had at last begun the dialogue about my sexual identity. It was such a huge relief and in retrospect, a giant first step in acknowledging who I was. A favorite saying of one of my colleagues rang in my ears—an experience is never complete until you have reflected upon it. The reflection had begun and no doubt would continue, but it wouldn't deepen without more experiences to feed it. I sealed the envelope, popped it into the mailbox outside the hostel, and went to buy antiseptic cream.

* * *

While parks and gardens were popular meeting places for men seeking sex with other men in India, suburban trains and railway stations were also fertile ground. Bombay's notoriously overcrowded trains lent themselves to all kinds of mischief, not least the infamous 'Eve teasing' women were subjected to. But at rush hour, in particular, opportunities for interpersonal contact abounded. I soon learned that certain carriages on certain trains were renowned for their furtive sexual activity. 'Adam teasing' I called it. Whenever returning home alone from an appointment, I would ferret out these carriages and try my luck. It was a game of Russian roulette. If it backfired, I could be in serious trouble. But as I graduated from bumbling amateur to sophisticated pro, the temptation to add another prize to my collection of diverse sexual conquests outweighed the risks.

My initiation into the wild ways of train sex happened most unexpectedly. Several weeks earlier I had met a young man who said he performed classical Bharatanatyam dance in hotels and clubs. He invited me to a performance, so one afternoon between appointments I decided to take up his offer. Posing as a hotel guest, I wangled my way into an auditorium at the Taj Palace Hotel and sat in the back. I'd always harbored a secret passion for dance but had never pursued it in the heavily macho society in which I grew up. So in a place where such expression by men was culturally acceptable, I felt like I could indulge my fantasy. I watched mesmerized by the elegance of his twirling arabesques and the pounding stutter of his feet. After he came off stage, I intercepted him on his way to his dressing room. His face was dripping with perspiration but his eyes lit up when he saw me.

'So you came! I never thought you would. But I'm so sorry. I can't stop now. Can you come to my house Saturday evening? I gave you my address, isn't it?'

I promised I would go. All week I could think only of meeting him again. By the time I boarded the train at Byculla station on Saturday evening, I was already turned on. I pushed my way into a carriage of wall-to-wall people and wriggled through the sea of bodies towards the rear of the car to avoid the crowds that surged through the doors at every stop. I reached up and grabbed a handle hanging from the ceiling to steady myself. Once it picked up speed, the train swayed with a gentle lilt, causing bodies to press against one another in a rhythmic motion. I stood trapped in front of a thickset young man, our legs touching each other. As the train moved and I rubbed up against him, I could feel myself getting hard. At first I was embarrassed and hoped my rising excitement would abate. Then I noticed when the train slowed and stopped swaying, the pressure between us didn't decrease. Far from objecting to my presence, this guy was encouraging it. I threw him a quick glance and he raised his eyebrows.

As soon as the train pulled out of the next station, he reached down, undid my fly, and slipped his hand inside my trousers. I was terrified other passengers would notice and sound the alarm. But another part of me was cheering him on. It didn't take long for him to claim victory. As the train began to slow for the next station, he gently withdrew his sticky hand from my trousers and made a halfhearted attempt to zip me up. His audacity floored me. I took a deep breath and tried to calm my nerves. Apparently my accomplice had acted just in time, since this seemed to be his stop. As he started moving towards the exit, he looked me firmly in the eye and cocked his head, urging me to follow him. I was sorely tempted but decided I would not renege on my dancer friend, who promised even greater rewards. As he melted into the billowing crowd on the platform, I wondered what this stranger thought about our encounter. For me, it was another one for the trophy room.

I soon learned that railway stations were also places of heavy activity for men looking for a quick release or a casual pick-up. Rumor had it that particular stations, even particular platforms on particular stations—and particular times of the day and night—were white-hot centers for contact. The focal point of activity was the men's urinal. At Dadar station, where the two main north–south lines converged and trains came and went by the minute, activity was brisk. This was certainly the case in the men's loo on number two platform, which one of my gay friends affectionately referred to as 'the temple.' Between about 6 pm and 11 pm any day of the week, waves of devotees could be seen entering its sacred walls to pay homage to the great god, instant male sex. Unfortunately, police officers also made regular visits, so I tended to give this shrine a wide berth.

However, other stations, purportedly less risky, did arouse my curiosity. One was Bombay Central, a major station on the suburban rail network as well as on the national grid. One evening returning home late, I decided to stop at Bombay Central to see if I might enliven what had been a rather dull day. The station clock registered 11.15 pm and the platforms were quiet. Trains came and went at growing intervals. As my train dribbled to a halt, I skipped onto the platform with the aplomb of a born-and-bred Bombay-wallah. After a quick reconnoiter, I made for the overhead bridge and descended to the middle platform where there was a men's lavatory. Something about the situation disturbed me, but I couldn't put my finger on it. Perhaps it just lacked the normal frenzied activity I'd become accustomed to. The echo of my own footsteps on the stone platform was strangely unsettling. I slowed down as I approached the toilet entrance, in half a mind to turn around and call it quits. But knowing when to walk away from a situation was something I'd never been good at.

As I stepped through the open doorway, the stench of urine overpowered me but I managed to put my revulsion on hold. There were two other patrons in the urinal, one at each end, so I positioned myself in the middle and glanced to my right and left. The older man to my left ignored me but the young man to my right made immediate eye contact. He looked down at my crotch, before reverting to his own. I took a slight nod of his head to be my invitation. My evening wasn't going to be such a dead end after all. As I leaned over to touch him, the older man turned and grabbed me.

'You are under arrest. Come with us.'

His words reverberated in my head like multiple gun shots. This couldn't be happening to me. This was the kind of thing that happened to Oscar Wilde or Alan Turing or thousands of other men in another time and place. Not me. Not now. How could I have been so foolish? Why hadn't I trusted my sixth sense and aborted my mission? There was no chance of running or fighting my way out of it this time.

I followed the two men to the main platform where they told me to sit down on a bench outside their office.

'What is your name?' asked the younger one.

I hesitated for a second while I debated how to reply.

'Graham Hawke,' I volunteered, merging the names of two close friends.

'Where you live?'

I dared not tell them, lest they trace me and contact the Institute.

'I don't live here. I'm visiting India.'

'Where you stay?'

'A small hotel in Colaba. I can't remember the name.'

Given the number of cheap tourist hotels in that part of the city, many of which were unregistered businesses, this was a reasonable answer. He switched his line of attack.

'You are breaking the law.'

I had half a mind to ask him which particular law, but thought better of it. How about laws against undercover police tactics? I held my tongue and let him dictate the next move. In this game we were playing, he held all the winning cards.

'You must pay 500 rupees or go to police station.'

My stomach tightened. I knew it would come down to money and I knew I didn't have a chance of paying. The idea of going to friends for a loan was so humiliating I couldn't entertain it. But spending time in a police lockup and having to explain my absence to my colleagues was even more unthinkable.

'I don't have 500 rupees,' I protested.

My interrogator looked over at his sidekick and mumbled in Marathi. Immediately, the older man approached me, yanked my body to an upright position, and searched me thoroughly. He extracted 25 rupees from my trouser pocket and waved it in front of his colleague's face as if to say, 'All this trouble for this much!'

'You come to police station now!' ordered the younger one.

A sense of dread overcame me. I needed to come up with something and fast. Then I remembered the emergency money I kept in a small plastic bag in my shoe. It wasn't much but it was worth a try. I bent down to take off my right shoe.

'What you doing?' he demanded.

'You want baksheesh?'

I slipped off my unlaced shoe but before I could take hold of the plastic bag, the officer saw it and grabbed it. He unfolded a 50-rupee note and slipped it into his shirt pocket.

'This all?' he asked.

Before I could answer, he pulled off my other shoe but found it contained nothing. He turned to his offsider and uttered a few rapid-fire Marathi sentences. I held my breath. Then without warning the officer turned to me and switched to English.

'Go,' he said, dismissing me with the flick of his wrist.

I couldn't believe my ears. Satisfied they had milked me for all I was worth, I was of no further interest to them. I considered making a run for it before they changed their minds, but decorum got the better of me. I strode away, trying valiantly to hold my head high as if to salvage some modicum of dignity. With not a paisa for bus fare, I exited the station and started walking towards Byculla.

* * *

It was standard practice in our organization to visit private companies, government offices or potential donors in pairs—one Indian and one foreigner. I had never questioned the wisdom of such a policy but as my yearning for sexual diversion increased, I started to finagle ways to cover more appointments on my own—it was only a follow-up call to nudge along a donation, or the donor had a penchant for foreigners. I was careful not to make too much of an issue of this lest I raise suspicions. It never occurred to me that some already harbored suspicions and were just waiting for me to commit a major indiscretion.

On a warm June afternoon, I waltzed out our front door and took the steps two at a time. With a nod to Charlie at the main gate, I crossed Sankli Street and headed for Byculla railway station. Even the stench of rotting mangoes from the fruit and vegetable market didn't affect me like it normally did. I hadn't felt like this since the incident at Bombay Central and my scrape with the police on the maidan. I had reduced my nightly forays and made an effort to spend more time socializing with coworkers to help me regain a sense of balance in my increasingly erratic life. Now that I was back on a more even keel, the urge to immerse myself in India's gay underground began to reassert itself.

When I turned the corner before the station, I saw him. He was about 20 meters ahead of me, walking in my direction. At first, he didn't stand out among dozens of others. Slightly built and of short stature, he wore the same white pants and cotton kurta as hundreds of others on this street. But as he came closer, something about his probing eyes triggered an immediate response in me.

As the gap between us narrowed, I tried to keep focused on his face while I battled the surging crowd. I lost sight of him fleetingly and when I looked up, he was almost in front of me. For the briefest moment our eyes locked in a glint of recognition. I kept walking a few paces, then turned my head. He did the same. I slowed down and checked back. He was moving away but just as I thought he was about to disappear into the crowd, he turned around again and stopped. We both stood transfixed, while people flowed around us. Then, as if on cue, we started walking towards each other. We came face to face and he looked into my eyes knowingly. A feeling of deep connection rippled through me. It was like a scene in a Bollywood movie, but it was utterly real. I stood paralyzed, not knowing what to say or do.

'You live around here?' he asked. 'I think I've seen you before.'

'Just on the other side of Byculla Bridge. I come this way to catch the train. Where do you stay?'

'Three doors down only.' Then barely without pausing he asked, 'Would you like to take tea?'

Refusing his invitation was not an option, as it rarely is when this question is asked in India. It has little to do with drinking a particular beverage and everything to do with having a chat, getting acquainted, or warming up to a business transaction. In this case, it felt like a proposition in the making.

Pointing to the Bharat Hotel across the road, my acquaintance led the way and chose a table in a far corner. Eyes followed us from around the room, since a foreigner was still an object of curiosity in this part of the city. A pani-wallah no more than nine or ten years old approached us with two glasses of cloudy-looking water and slammed them down before us.

The waiter then came to take our order. 'Waiter' is too refined a term for these young men who work in hotels and restaurants virtually as bonded labor. They eat and sleep on the premises, earning a few rupees a day and often suffer degrading sexual and physical abuse. But this waiter still had a spark of life left in him. He looked at my companion as if to say, 'Don't think I don't know what you are up to.' My friend commanded 'Do chai!' and the young man scuttled away to fetch our tea.

'So where are you from?' he asked. 'England or America?' Obviously, I hadn't said enough for him to catch my antipodean roots, or my English had become so Indianized he couldn't detect its origins.

'Neither. Australia.'

'Oh, really? You don't sound Australian. What are you doing in India?'

I pressed the button to activate my standard spiel.

'And you,' I inquired, 'are you a student?'

'How did you know?'

Those books under your arm…'

'Yes, I'm doing pre-med. At JJ Hospital. Have you heard of it?'

I admitted I had. I passed it practically every day.

As I readjusted my focus on the young man sitting across from me, I realized how exquisite his features were—an angular face with a gently hooked nose, impeccable white teeth, jet black hair loosely parted to one side, deep-set dark brown eyes and rich caramel skin so unblemished compared to the blotchy, sunburnt varieties I'd grown up with. All this and a gently sculpted figure to boot—made to order.

I'd come across many Indian men whose natural beauty enraptured me, but to find someone to whom I was attracted physically and with whom I could converse on topics other than sex was a rarity. I looked at my watch. I would be late for my appointment if I didn't leave shortly, so I began to excuse myself.

'My name is John. And you are?'

'I'm Pratap. Let me give you my phone number. You can call me at home most evenings.'

Things were moving faster than I had anticipated. After so many nights fruitlessly cruising the maidan or the Bandstand, I'd met someone within a few hundred meters of home whom I genuinely liked and wanted to pursue.

We swapped phone numbers, and after he insisted on paying for the tea we politely shook hands. I don't know what made me do it, but clasping his hand, I tickled his palm with my forefinger—something I'd learned at the Bandstand. Without hesitation, he returned the favor.

Over the next six months, Pratap and I met whenever we

could, between my trips to other parts of the country and the demands of his medical studies. The first time he invited me to his home was a memorable occasion. Pratap alerted me that since I was their first foreign guest, his mother was nervous that I would not like her food she had spent hours preparing. But she need not have worried. Many invitations to village homes had taught me about being a polite guest, even when the food was so riddled with chili I had no idea what I was eating. In contrast, her flavorful egg curry, pan-hot chapattis and cucumber raita were a sheer delight. After she attempted to refill my plate for the third time, I smiled appreciatively but waved my hands to indicate that I had reached my limit.

'Oh bai, khaana bahut achchha hai!' I exclaimed as she offered me a finger bowl with lemon to wash my hands.

My compliments to the chef didn't go unnoticed. She looked at Pratap, wide-eyed, and said something to him. He turned to me and explained that his mother was very happy that I liked her food. 'Not half as happy as I am about liking her son!' I shot back, causing Pratap to blush. His low-key, reserved nature in the presence of his mother touched me. Deference towards parents and seniors was something I had come to respect in India. When we retreated to Pratap's room after the meal, we couldn't bring ourselves to engage in sex, with his mother only meters away on the other side of the door. We decided to go to a movie instead.

Since neither of us was a fan of formulaic blockbuster movies, we chose an art film. Bombay has hundreds of cinemas, some seedy and run-down and others quite grand establishments, even if the worse for wear. This fell under that category. We bought our tickets and headed for the back stalls. The theater was about three-quarters full but the seats on either side of us were vacant, and those behind us only sparsely occupied. I breathed a sigh of relief. Finding a seat in an Indian cinema not surrounded by other patrons was rare.

The air-conditioning was cool enough for me to take off my light jacket and put it across my legs. Pratap followed suit. About 10 minutes into the picture, I moved my leg a little to the left, brushing his ever so gently. I felt a nudge from him in return. We both kept looking straight ahead but our attention was not on the drama on the screen. I let my leg rest on his for a few minutes then decided to push my luck a little further. I gently put my hand on his thigh and felt him take a deep breath. His leg continued to press against mine. I slowly slid my hand over and felt between his legs. I could hardly believe we were doing this. I looked out the corner of my eye to see if we were being observed but everyone nearby seemed engrossed in the movie. Without moving my head, I felt for the tag at the top of his zipper and ever so slowly pulled it down. I slid my hand inside his pants and held him firmly. I didn't have to do any more.

I let out a slow, controlled sigh. I could feel him relax too, allowing the wonder of the moment to sink in. For a few seconds, we both basked in the glow of our audacious act. Then I sensed his anxiety growing. The embarrassment of being caught *in flagrante delicto* was more than he could bear. He indicated for me to withdraw my hand. As I did, I glanced at him and he threw me a gentle smile.

***

Six months passed before we met again, this time in more relaxing circumstances. It was a lucky chance that made it possible. I was part of a team of facilitators leading a strategic planning course with an Indian company at a five-star hotel at Bombay airport. Staying in such lavish surroundings was a rarity that I relished to the full. I took several hot showers, indulged myself in exotic delicacies from the French restaurant, and felt duty-bound to relieve the hotel of its imported toiletries. These things in themselves might have been cause for celebration, but having a room to myself was pure, unadulterated heaven.

I wondered who I could call at such short notice to help me take advantage of it. After my last meeting with Naresh on the train to Delhi, he was certainly not an option. Pratap was the one I really wanted to share an evening with, although the chance he'd be available at such short notice was slim. I picked up the receiver and dialed. His mother answered and recognized my name. My Hindi left me wanting and I was about to hang up the phone when Pratap came on the line. I explained my situation and he said he'd be there in about an hour.

I feverishly prepared myself for his arrival. I showered for the third time that day and doused myself with my favorite jasmine after-shave. I tried reading but was so filled with anticipation that I was unable to concentrate on the words. The phone rang and I grabbed the receiver.

'Hey Burbs, you joining the rest of us in the lounge for one last drink?'

'Thanks, Sean, but I think I'll give it a miss. Must be those snails I had for dinner. I'm not feeling too good. I'll have to pass.'

My lame excuse seemed to do the trick and he backed off, but not before adding, 'Watch out for those guys on room service.' Did he know more than I thought?

The promised hour came and went. Another thirty minutes went by. I grew worried and called Pratap's number again. His mother answered and said something about meeting a friend. I thanked her for the news and tried to relax. I must have dozed off, for I was awoken by a light rat-a-tat. I jumped out of bed and rushed to the door.

It was Pratap, all in white looking as angelic as ever. He slipped in quietly and glanced in my direction.

'I'm sorry I can't stay long,' he apologized.

'No worries. Let's enjoy while we can.'

He began to take off his kurta, but I shook my head.

'No Pratap. Allow me the pleasure of disrobing my Indian prince.'

He laughed but acquiesced to my request. I peeled off the layers of his clothing until all that was left was the sacred thread Hindu men tie around their waists. With a gentle pull, I drew him towards me and we sank down into the waiting bed. As I did so, I was overcome by an image I'd seen on an ancient temple— two bodies entwined as one, a blissful serenity on their faces. I was gripped by its power and surrendered to it.

COLLISION COURSE

Several things distinguished our organization from many others working in community development, but one of the most remarkable was its capacity to think big and act upon its vision with unbridled passion and commitment. Since its beginnings in the black ghetto of Chicago, this had been a hallmark of the Institute. In the early 1980s, it embarked upon one of its most ambitious schemes ever—an international exposition of rural development, the culmination of which was a 10-day gathering in India in early 1984.

Spread over several years with lead-up events in many countries, the exposition brought together those engaged in the daily grind of grassroots development to share what they had learned. It was not another talkfest of academics and donors ruminating on the finer points of development theory. It was a hands-on exchange by local people and those who worked shoulder to shoulder with them, to highlight how the rural poor have succeeded in lifting themselves out of misery and deprivation. Seminar papers and symposia gave way to participatory workshops and site visits. More than 600 people from 55 countries came to India. In multinational teams, they traveled the length and breadth of the country by plane, train, bus, jeep and bullock cart to 35 chosen projects. For three days they walked, talked, ate and celebrated with their Indian hosts. The opening and closing events were held in New Delhi.

The exposition required immense preparation. As organizing sponsor, the Institute found itself called upon to make a quantum leap in its internal operations and public exposure. It was granted UN consultative status and lifted its fundraising bar to new heights. Although staff all over the world were engaged in the task, it fell to those of us in India to do the lion's share of the work. For me, it meant more travel, meeting more people in higher echelons of Indian society, and playing more conspicuous and weighty public roles than I had ever done before. I also happened to be at my most sexually active and was willing to risk myself more than I had ever dared. It was like being on two fast-moving trains going on the same track but in opposite directions. Sooner or later, a collision was bound to occur.

The fundraising team I was a part of was comprised of Indians and foreigners of both sexes. The Indians were Hindu, Muslim and Christian, and the foreigners came from Australia, Canada and the US. All were under 35 years of age, some more experienced than others. We operated in teams in different parts of the country, although their members changed from time to time. I often partnered with young Indian men who had come from villages and who had to work hard to assert themselves in the sophisticated world of Indian business. When a foreigner and an Indian showed up in the office of a corporate executive, the foreigner was invariably shown more respect than his Indian colleague. Sometimes, the Indian was taken to be the foreigner's assistant and treated accordingly. If one chair was available, it would be given to the foreigner. When tea was brought in, the foreigner would be served first. When questions were asked, they were almost always directed to the foreigner. I was continually searching for ways to counter these habits without offending the person whose support we were soliciting.

I knew some of these young men from earlier years when we had worked in villages together. Manoj and I had shared responsibility for a cluster of village projects in eastern Maharashtra. Day in and day out, battling the stifling heat and choking dust of the bone-dry landscape, we would buffet our way onto overcrowded State Transport buses, visit offices of the District Commissioner or the local Block Development Officer, and sleep side by side on the rock-hard, dung floor of a wattle-and-daub hut. We ate the same repetitive rice and dal, lived on the same paltry monthly stipends, and led village meetings together. I appreciated the huge leap it was for these young men to move from a familiar rural environment to the alien world of India's cities, a world in which I felt more at home than they did.

Part of my respect for them led me to draw a firm line in the sand when it came to my sexual interests. Although some of my young colleagues were attractive, I never allowed myself to imagine them as sexual partners, let alone act upon such feelings. It was as if we were brothers or cousins in a large, extended family and as such, sexual intimacy was not an option. I was also aware of the cultural gap that existed between villager and urban dweller, especially in matters like homosexuality. I never expected my village colleagues to understand what it would mean to be a gay man in India, since they'd probably never known one. Besides, I was finding more than ample opportunities for making friends outside the organization.

Living life in two fast lanes simultaneously, I wasn't always aware of the subtle shifts taking place around me. Whether due to naiveté or denial, I carried on with my double life as though no one noticed or cared, neither of which I would discover was true. Perhaps that is why I never questioned why I began to be assigned to work more with the female members of our team, particularly the Indian women. I liked them; we enjoyed life on the road together and made an unusual team that intrigued those we met. There was no question of me posing a threat to their womanhood—undoubtedly a significant consideration for Henry while allocating assignments. It may also have been his way of trying to divert me from the wayward path he was convinced I was on. In our first year of working and living together, Henry and I had managed to coexist on mutually agreeable terms but midway through our second year, the strain of thin-skinned toleration began to show.

One event may well have hastened our inevitable confrontation. It was mid-morning and our team was gathered in our office to report on recent trips around the country. Sushila entered the room and announced that Henry had visitors at the front door. Not one to be deflected from his task, he told her to ask them to wait for a few minutes until we took a break. When he eventually went to greet these mysterious visitors, he returned right away with a frown on his forehead and made straight for me.

'It's you they want to see,' he said curtly. 'Some friends of yours from Calcutta.'

The disingenuous way he said 'friends' caused me to seize up. Given my growing array of contacts in Calcutta, these friends could have been any number of people, although I was careful about revealing my Bombay address. As I made my way to the front porch, my stomach turned over in anxious anticipation. At first, I didn't recognize our two guests. Then it came to me. I had met the younger man at the Calcutta maidan several months before and we'd had a fleeting sexual affair. He was unemployed and said he had relatives in Bombay, and was thinking of coming here in search of work. In a moment of magnanimity, I had offered to try to help him. His was a common story, so I'd paid little attention to it at the time. I couldn't even recall his name. I had never dreamed that he would show up on my doorstep and certainly didn't think he would bring a family member in tow. It felt like I was caught in a vise of my own making.

'You said you would help me find a job in Bombay,' my young friend remarked, cutting to the chase. Then glancing at his companion, he added, 'My uncle said he would like to meet you.'

'Namaste,' I said, with a polite nod to the older man. 'Does your uncle understand English?'

'Thoda thoda,' he replied.

For this I was grateful, because I feared I might be in for quite a grilling. I wasn't sure whether this conversation was actually about helping my friend find a job or his attempt to blackmail me over our sexual liaison, should I not deliver on my promise.

I apologized for not being able to offer them chai and made excuses about having to return to my meeting, all the while groping for a way to get them to leave as quickly as possible.

'What kind of job are you looking for?' I asked.

'Office job.'

'What qualifications do you have?'

'B. Com,' he mumbled.

Bachelors of Commerce in India were a dime a dozen. He was competing with millions of others in the labor market and without some kind of clout there was little chance he would reach even the lowest rung of the corporate ladder. He was hoping I might provide that clout. As I was about to respond, one of my team members entered the porch.

'Henry is asking for you,' she said, eyeing my two visitors suspiciously.

'Tell him I'll be right there.'

This provided me with the out I was looking for. I promised the young man I would do my best to see if anyone I knew had an opening for him, but asked him not to return. I also asked him for his uncle's address and phone number so I could initiate further contact.

'I'll get in touch with you in a week,' I promised blithely.

The older man looked surprised that this was the end of our meeting. Obviously, his nephew had led him to expect more. I hoped this would be the last I would see of his uncle but I had my doubts. Exactly what had the young man told him about me? Would I regret our liaison and my glib offer of assistance? I would need to be much more careful in future. I stood up, namasted, and walked back into our office.

Try as I might to pretend that this was merely an annoying interruption, I couldn't help think otherwise. I began to wonder what kind of rumors had been circulating about me behind my back. How much did others suspect or know about my other life? As I sat down at the table and tried to refocus on the task at hand, Henry shot me a look that had 'gotcha' smeared all over it.

* * *

Going to Delhi from Bombay was like visiting another country, especially New Delhi, with its grand boulevards, monumental buildings and spacious shopping centers. Old Delhi was more of the same—serpentine alleyways, snarling traffic, and ancient bazaars where cinnamon incense and marigold garlands stood side by side with bags of basmati rice and mounds of golden turmeric. New Delhi, on the other hand, afforded certain luxuries that made the laborious overnight journey from Bombay worth the effort. Its proximity to the Punjab, home of India's green revolution, meant that milkshakes replaced milk rations and dairy products like cheese and ice-cream were readily available. The apple orchards of nearby Himachal Pradesh supplied the capital with fresh juice that was like nectar of the gods during the blasting heat of north Indian summers. And the rich chocolate-brown dal served in Delhi restaurants was a welcome change from the familiar yellow and red pulses that were a staple of our Maharashtrian diet.

It was August 1982, and with many staff members away at annual meetings work was at a low ebb, so I requested a week off to get to know the country's capital city, despite the scorching heat. I had been to Delhi several times but had had little chance to familiarize myself with its historic sites and national landmarks. Moreover, I had by now accumulated an impressive list of local referrals from gay friends around the country and was keen to become acquainted with them. In a letter to my mother shortly after my return to Bombay, I reported that I had 'got to know a bunch of new friends' but spared her the details of who, where and how. I didn't dare mention my frequent sorties to a large park adjacent to the diplomatic enclave, my tryst with a handsome medical student in his hostel room, or sharing a charpoy with another young man on the rooftop of his family home. It was a sensual fiesta that left me drooling for more. The dry summer heat only stoked my internal fires. By day, I added to my knowledge of India's prolific cultural heritage by probing the many layers of its history. By night, I hit the streets and parks.

But this was not all. The visit cracked the illusion I had developed that my sexual adventuring went unnoticed by others. It also revealed how amazingly interconnected the Indian gay community was, given its amorphous and secluded nature and its vast numbers. This came to me one evening at Connaught Place, a circular park in the heart of New Delhi and a popular gay hangout known to regulars as 'The Club'. I had done several rounds of the park and failing to find anyone who caught my eye, was about to leave when I noticed a figure hovering in the shadows of a clump of nearby trees. Now and then he would look in my direction, as if trying to catch my attention. We played cat and mouse while I decided whether or not to approach him. He finally took the decision out of my hands as he turned and came straight towards me.

'Is your name John?' he asked.

'Ah…yes,' I replied, wondering how on earth he could know.

'You are from Bombay?'

'Yes, I am.'

'Is your telephone number there 374921?'

I was stunned. Who was he? A private investigator? Plain-clothes CID? My heart began to thump.

'How do you know me?'

'I don't, but I've been trying to track you down for the past week,' he said with a sense of accomplishment. 'I was in Bombay and met a good friend of yours, Satish. He suggested we might enjoy getting to know each other so he gave me your number. When I phoned your place in Bombay, I was told you had gone to Delhi and was given your office number. I had to come here on family matters, so I tried calling you but your phone was out of order. When a friend said he'd heard that a gay foreigner from Bombay was visiting Delhi, I thought this was the most probable place to find you.'

I was flabbergasted. More than 10 million people in Bombay and over half that many in Delhi, and we just happened to run into each other, thanks to the gay grapevine. I felt uncomfortably conspicuous as I never had before in India. My name and reputation had begun to spread in ways that baffled and unnerved me. Any notion I had of anonymity had been shown the door. I berated myself for my lack of discretion, and made a mental note for the future. It was a timely caution, and one I needed to take heed of.

My emerging notoriety in India's vast gay underground was one thing. Of greater concern to me was the fact that my nightly sprees had begun to attract the attention of colleagues. I was aware of Henry's growing antagonism towards me, but I had no idea that other staff members also had qualms about my extra-curricular activities. One of these was Tarabai, the senior Indian woman in our Delhi office, a compact stone-and-plaster house that served as our base. During my next visit there, I was fortunate to be given a small room facing the courtyard at the back of house, which afforded me a little privacy from most of the staff. I quickly saw the advantage of this location and wondered how I might put it to good use.

On my first Saturday night there, our staff were invited to a reception at the Dutch Embassy, a prominent donor to our work in India. Tarabai insisted that I accompany them. Normally, I would not have passed up the chance to enjoy tasty European hors d'oeuvres and down a few cold Heinekens, but on this occasion I had a more enticing choice on my menu. Ravindra, a robust Punjabi who worked as a trainee manager in a five-star hotel, had told me it was his night off and we had agreed to meet. I planned to wait until the rest of the staff had left for the embassy and then bring Ravindra back to my room. I knew he couldn't stay over but most probably he would be gone before my colleagues returned.

'You are going to join us at the reception tonight,' said Tarabai, half-answer, half-question.

'Well, actually, I have other plans,' I replied. 'A friend has invited me out to dinner. Sorry.'

'It would be really good for you to be there. The Dutch have been one of our major supporters and have been most useful opening doors for the exposition also.'

'That's true, but I don't have the main contact with them.

The Delhi staff have cultivated the relationship. I'd be just another face.'

'Not just another face. I think you'd be a very helpful face. We could do with some other nationalities than Indians and Americans around here.'

She wasn't backing down, so I needed to play a different card. I decided to go for a feint and save my thrust for later.

'Well, I'll think about it. My friend asked me to dinner some time ago and I don't wish to disappoint him. He's also extremely interested in our work and would like to help in some way.'

I'm not sure where my last sentence came from, although there was a tiny shred of truth in it. But once I'd said it, it planted an idea in my mind. I called Ravindra and told him my predicament. He offered to cancel our date but I was adamant he didn't. Instead, I asked him to come to our place earlier than we had planned so I could introduce him to our staff.

'You sure that's a good idea?' he asked.

'Oh, yes, once they meet you and see that you are genuinely interested in what we do, they will not be so suspicious, not even Tarabai.'

My trust in others' good faith knew no bounds. By taking the offensive and introducing my friend to my colleagues, I felt sure Tarabai would stop insisting I come to the reception. She could hardly demand that I renege on my guest in front of him.

When Ravindra arrived, smartly dressed in a dark blue Nehru shirt, I knew he would make a good impression. He was polite and articulate with his smooth, educated English.

Management training in the hotel trade had left its mark on him. He engaged Tarabai in conversation rather than waiting for her to ask the questions. What more could I have hoped for? When it came time for our staff to leave for the embassy, I made my move.

'If you'll excuse us now, we must be going,' I addressed the group.

'You sure you won't join us?' came Tarabai's final riposte. 'Ravindra would be welcome too.'

I thought I had outsmarted her but she was calling checkmate. I looked at Ravindra and he looked back at me. He could see I was desperate and came to my rescue.

'Thank you for the invitation, but I'm afraid I cannot stay. I have arranged for us to have dinner with a friend and then I must go home.'

He was brilliant. I waited until all the staff had left before returning to Ravindra in the courtyard. I led him by the hand to my nook of a room and locked the door.

Tarabai's unusually persistent manner bothered me. Surely, it wasn't my presence at a run-of-the-mill social function that was the issue. Such events were a regular part of the Delhi scene, even for non-governmental organizations like ours. There had to be more to it. Colleagues would comment on my ability to make contacts outside the organization and win them over to our cause. But Tarabai's reaction to Ravindra was different. It was as though she would go to any length to ensure we didn't spend time alone together.

***

I would make other trips to Delhi, but more often I found

myself assigned to Calcutta, on the eastern edge of the country. Situated on the lower reaches of the Ganges, this one-time jewel in the British colonial crown had disintegrated into an urban miasma that defied imagination. Crowds gathered daily in one of the main public squares to stare in fascination as hundreds of rats scurried about in their burrowed colony. Rickshaw-wallahs did battle with Ambassador taxis, bullock carts, scooters and pedestrians along potholed streets. The dissonance of blaring horns, shrieking voices and bellowing animals was punctuated by the frequent clanging of bells, as ancient trams shuffled their way from one corner of the city to another, devouring their human cargo at one stop and spewing it out at the next. Subject to constant power outages, sweltering humidity and deluging monsoon rains, it was a city that, to a naïve outsider, had ceased to function at all. Mother Teresa and the Eden Gardens cricket ground notwithstanding, the city attracted little outside attention. But for native Bengalis, Calcutta was that without which life would not be worth living. For me, after the initial shock and disorientation had subsided, it became a most precious place.

While the city center left much to be desired, the surrounding suburbs dotted with parks and lakes offered a welcome alternative. But it was in the congested backstreets of Calcutta's sprawling bustees where the poorer and less fortunate lived, that the city's heartbeat could be most easily felt. As a hand-painted billboard proudly proclaimed, 'Calcutta Lives on Calcutta Itself.' This indomitable spirit was evident throughout the bustees. Thousands of local self-help organizations, from English classes to papadam kitchens, sprouted in homes and sheds along the alleyways. It was on one of these lanes that our staff of several families rented the downstairs of a two-story house that doubled as our office and residence. Taxi drivers were always surprised when delivering international visitors to our lane. No foreigner, except perhaps volunteers for the Sisters of Charity and the odd drug-addicted soul, would live in such a place. In spite of our oddity, we came to be accepted as part of this community. It was a short walk to nearby Park Circus market with its cheap restaurants and shops selling sweet curd and syrupy rasgulla that few Bengalis could resist.

One of the pleasures of coming to Calcutta for me had to do with our staff. This mix of Indians and foreigners, including singles, couples and one family with three young children was typical of our other centers, but the mood here was markedly different. It was more relaxed and upbeat, with joking and teasing a standard routine. Squeezed between the landlady's apartment above and the alleyway right outside the front door, the living and working space was even more cramped than in Bombay, but the genial atmosphere more than compensated for the restrictive conditions. This could be attributed to the directors, Sean and Sandy, the husband and wife duo who set the tone of the place. Sean's Irish American sardonic humor and Sandy's bubbly warmth and English charm were an enticing combination. Even when he called her 'pig face' in a public meeting, we all knew that this was nothing more than a perverse term of endearment. Along with everyone else, I came in for my fair share of ribbing and soon learned the knack of give and take. Perhaps this was one reason why I tended to let down my guard more when in Calcutta and push the boundaries of my nocturnal explorations.

This time, however, work absorbed most of my energy and three weeks in Calcutta flew by. I helped our local staff secure commitments for more than 100,000 rupees or $10,000 USD but most of my time was spent visiting Indian companies, convincing them to buy advertising space in the exposition brochure. On my return, my luggage was noticeably heavier than it had been on the outward journey, since it contained a number of lead printing blocks. I was also carrying two large jars of pickles I had bought in the old city market, one of which was for Henry, who had asked that I bring him back one of his favorite delicacies. I made sure I didn't forget his request, since it could only help improve our increasingly strained relationship. This gesture, coupled with our best-ever month of fundraising in Calcutta, made the prospect of returning to Bombay more attractive than usual.

On the day of my departure, I made a point of arriving at Howrah station an hour and a half ahead of time. Since I had a reserved berth, I decided to head for the station cafeteria for a quick cup of tea and a masala dosa before boarding. When I headed out onto the platform 45 minutes later, the crowd seemed to have grown tenfold. So too had the level of yelling and screaming by impatient passengers, opportunistic porters, and ever-hopeful salesmen. Taking out my ticket, I proceeded to locate my carriage. As usual, the numbers of the carriages were scribbled on the side of the cars in chalk. On some carriages, they had been changed several times, so the result was a smudgy blur. What's more, the alphabetical numbering of the carriages wasn't sequential. I found carriages H and J but no I. I looked up at the station clock. Only 25 minutes remained before departure.

Battling the crowd, I gathered up my luggage and walked the entire length of the train again, sure that I would find my carriage this time. Alas, I didn't. A quiver of fear ripped through my body. How could it not be there? Did I have a ticket for the wrong day or the wrong train? I was sure neither was the case. I looked again at the clock. Less than 20 minutes to go. If worst came to worst, I would jump onto the nearest carriage and do my ignorant foreigner routine with the first ticket conductor I found. Trying to get near a conductor on the platform would require a substantial athletic feat. Tossing politeness aside, I barreled my way through the crowd surrounding one and shouted, 'Conductor sahib, please help me. I've gone up and down the train twice and I still can't find my carriage. I don't have much time left. Where is I-19?'

With a finely honed bureaucratic nonchalance derived from dealing with thousands of situations like this, the conductor ignored my plea and continued what he was doing. I repeated myself, louder.

'Can't you see I am busy?' he retorted. 'Wait your turn.'

'But conductor sahib, the train is about to leave!' I protested.

Not to be dismissed lightly, I thrust my hand in front of him and waved my ticket back and forth. The clock was ticking; my stomach was tightening. Then he suddenly turned towards me and grabbed the ticket from my hand. Glancing at it, he stated bluntly, 'This is down the other end of the train. You'll have to hurry.'

Garnering every ounce of energy I could muster, I grabbed my bags and made a wild dash down the platform. I ran the length of the platform, dodging bodies and animals, tea stands and banana-wallahs. Nearing the end of the platform, I heard the first of two whistles. Then the second whistle blew. It was now or never. This section of the train was unmistakably first class, for which I could not afford a ticket, even if by some rare miracle a seat was still available. First-class berths were much more expensive and usually booked well in advance. Desperate to catch the train, I jumped onto the nearest carriage and dropped my bag just inside the door. When a conductor eventually appeared, we were 40 minutes out of Howrah station. I showed him my ticket and tried to explain my situation. His eyes squinted and his brow furrowed.

'This is not a first-class ticket,' he exclaimed. 'Your carriage is far from here. You will have to wait until we reach Jamshedpur and I will have to take you. But you'll need to be quick because we only stop for a few minutes. We will be arriving in about an hour. Wait here.'

I plunked down on the floor and contemplated my situation. Nothing made sense. It had been such a good couple of weeks in Calcutta. For once, things were going my way. Surely my luck would continue a bit longer. But India had a unique capacity to raise you up to new heights then knock you down with deflating blows. It was something my logical mind could never fathom and over which I had no control. My life felt like an accordion, one moment being splayed apart and the next being squished together. Despite its excruciating demands, something about this concertinaed lifestyle was strangely energizing. Right now, my body and mind were in overdrive. I tried not to think of anything but the rolling motion of the train as it sped west. I only hoped the worst was over and that things would improve.

It was nearly 11 pm when the Gitanjali pulled into

Jamshedpur station. All I could see was the dimly lit platform against a pitch-black sky. In the distance a dog's bark broke the silence. As the train came to a halt, the conductor appeared and gestured to me to follow him. Our carriage was beyond the end of the platform, leaving a sizable gap between the bottom step and the ground. The conductor jumped down first and I passed him my luggage before leaping myself. I hit the earth with a thud and almost overbalanced.

'Hurry up!' he commanded, as he led the way at a brisk trot. I couldn't believe the train was so long. It seemed to have grown since I had examined it at Howrah station. The first whistle blew and the conductor motioned to me to go faster. With my overweight case, I could barely keep up with him. Right as the second whistle blew, he pointed to a carriage door and motioned me to get up. I glanced up to where the carriage number was meant to be. All I could see was a chalky smudge.

As I tried to catch my breath, he pushed past me and began checking seat numbers. When he reached number 19, he found another body occupying it. With a thunderous voice, the conductor ordered the man out of the berth and told me to take it. The departing passenger glared at me and muttered something under his breath. What others thought I could only conjecture, but didn't much care. I was exhausted and only wanted to sleep.

My berth was a lower one parallel to the direction of the train, next to the door at the end of the carriage. Due to my late arrival, there was no space for my luggage in the overhead racks, so I was forced to put it under my seat. As I did so, an older man from the compartment opposite came over to me.

'You should be careful putting your case so close to the

door,' he said. 'It would be easy for someone to take it. You can store it with us if you like.'

I was taken aback by his offer and hesitated for a second or two. Was it genuine or was it a ruse to get his hands on my luggage? My extensive train travel in India had taught me to keep my luggage within sight and hand's reach at all times. Deciding to err on the side of caution, I thanked the man but said I would prefer to keep it close to me. He looked at me askance, shrugged his shoulders, and returned to his compartment. But his advice wasn't entirely wasted. I stowed the case under the berth at the end farthest from the door. As I did so, I was reminded how heavy it was with its printers' blocks, jars of pickles, and my beloved shortwave radio among other things. Its weight alone was a disincentive to any light-fingered visitor.

In spite of all I'd been through in the last several hours—or maybe because of it—it took me a long while to get to sleep. I was conscious of the train stopping several times during the night, and each time I reached down under my berth and touched my case to make sure it was there. But in the early hours of the morning I must have dozed off. Only after Kalyan, the last stop before Bombay, I woke up. I was surprised so many people were moving about the carriage, since usually the slightest noise or movement was enough to awaken me.

Instinctively, I lowered my hand and waved it around. Nothing was there. I rolled over and looked beneath my berth. There was a gaping space. I wanted to scream out a loud 'No!' It couldn't be true. How was it possible for someone to take my case out from under me without my knowing? Thank goodness I had put my money and passport in my satchel under my pillow.

While I was still trying to grasp what had happened, the man from the compartment opposite came over and sat down. He was sympathetic to my plight but with an 'I-told-you-so' look in his eye. He invited me to join his family for chai and insisted that I put my remaining case with their luggage, even though we were only a short distance from Bombay. At this point, I could take all the kindness I could get.

As the train snaked its way through the outlying areas of the city, the suffocating heat of the lower elevation engulfed me. Looking out the window, I watched the early morning diorama that accompanies railway lines in India. But unlike on my outward journey several weeks before, none of this human drama was of the least interest to me, not even the occasional glimpse of a temptingly muscular body taking a bucket bath. All I could think of was the loss of my case and how I would break the news to my colleagues. At least they would be sympathetic.

Instead of wallowing in self-pity, I resolved to do something. As soon as the train pulled into Victoria Terminus, I went straight to the Railway Police and lodged a complaint for stolen property. The duty officer didn't blink an eyelid as I related my tale of woe. He must have heard thousands of stories like it, especially from naïve foreigners.

'You do one thing,' he commanded. 'Fill out this form and sign it.'

He pushed a yellowing piece of paper in front of me. It looked to be the same form some punctilious British civil servant had designed a couple of centuries before. I knew that filling it out was futile. It was an empty bureaucratic procedure that would end up in a file that over time would be shredded by rats or cockroaches in some moldy storage room. At least it created the illusion that I was doing something to address my sorry situation.

But I was still not ready to face my colleagues. An odd mix of shame and guilt overcame me. I needed time to rehearse my story and compose myself. I headed for the station dining room and ordered my favorite 'full breakfast'—a hangover from British times that could still be found in some Indian railway stations. Between the imitation cornflakes and greasy fried eggs, I couldn't hold back the tears any longer. They began as a trickle but within moments, I was sobbing uncontrollably. I couldn't remember when I had last done this, if ever. Not letting my emotions show was something I'd become skilled at, even prided myself on. I was embarrassed others would notice but few people were in the room. As I reached down in my pocket and pulled out my handkerchief, I pushed my plate away and let the tears take their course.

FRIENDS AND FIENDS

The sense of accomplishment I had experienced when I left Calcutta had been replaced by a confusing mixture of shame, guilt and loss by the time I returned to Bombay.

I decided to go straight to our office and tell my story, since I was sure it would help to share it with someone.

'Ah, Mr. John is back!' beamed Manoj. 'So how was the "Far East"?'

I cleared my throat as I tried to stick to our old adage, 'always state the positive before the negative.'

'Well, we had our best month ever. We raised over one lakh rupees,' I proudly proclaimed.

'Vah. Arrey baap rey!' exclaimed Manoj.

Henry looked up, as if he was about to speak.

'But I ran into problems on the way home. I was robbed on the Gitanjali and lost my pilot's case, with all the advertising blocks I picked up in Calcutta. Not to mention my radio and two jars of pickles.'

Henry stood up from his chair and walked over to me.

'How many blocks did you lose?'

'Seven or eight, I think.'

'Shit! We were counting on those. You know what that means, don't you? We're going to have to get replacements and delay the publication date even further. Damn!'

I glanced at Manoj. The look of disbelief on his face only reinforced my own shock at Henry's response. No acknowledgement of our most successful fundraising month ever in Calcutta. No compassion for my personal misfortune. Not even an inquiry about the nature of the mishap. I was tempted to retaliate but couldn't find the words that would come close to expressing my anger. I turned and stormed out of the room. Grabbing my satchel, I raced downstairs, out the front gate, and down to the corner of Clare Road to one of my favorite cafés. Slumping into a chair, I ordered chai while trying to figure out what to do. That Henry and I had to work together on the same team was bad enough; that we had to sleep in the same room was an anathema. I wasn't sure I could go on like that much longer. My mind overflowed with vengeful thoughts that demanded to be funneled into a plan of action. After his icy welcome, I was convinced we were headed for an impasse. I didn't have to wait long to have my intuition confirmed.

Two weeks after my return, our Bombay staff undertook 'tribal resettlement.' This custom was designed to ensure that no individual or family became too attached to their assigned space in our community. Sometimes this involved physically changing the temporary structures we had erectedbut mostly it meant shifting people from one room to another. Although it was inconvenient, tribal resettlement was strangely refreshing in the way that cleaning out a garage or reorganizing file drawers can be.

When the new housing plan was unveiled, I was greatly relieved to find that Henry and I had been assigned different rooms. Perhaps others were not so oblivious to the growing tension between us, or Henry had pulled some strings of his own. Either way, I was glad not to have to spend another night in the same room as him. There were, however, a couple of differences between our new arrangements. My 'room' was a narrow space, separated from the kitchen by a thin curtain and barely wide enough to fit a double bunk with a meter to spare on one side. Since I was away three weeks every month, such cramped quarters didn't bother me, but it made storage of clothes and other items difficult. Henry's space was not a lot larger but it contained a small closet and a chest of drawers. Much to my surprise, he offered me the use of one of his drawers.

However, given our past history, I wrote a short note declining his offer and left it on top of his dresser before I left for an appointment with Manoj. When we returned, we had only just entered the front door when Henry came marching down the corridor towards us. His beady eyes looked straight at me and his face reddened.

'You and I need to talk. Now. Downstairs.'

I felt like an errant schoolboy being ordered to the headmaster's office. I followed Henry to the ground floor and out into a corner of the compound.

'What's the meaning of this?' he demanded, thrusting my note in front of me. 'I offer to help you out and you insult me like this?'

'One drawer when you have the rest of the dresser is hardly unbounded generosity.'

'You should be grateful for what you can get, instead of turning your nose up at it.'

'I suppose I should be grateful for losing my luggage as well.'

'That's got nothing to do with this.'

'What has this got to do with, Henry?'

'Don't think I don't know what you've been up to every night.'

'And what would that be?'

'You know as well as I do, and if it doesn't stop, you'll find yourself reassigned.'

Was he really aware of my other life or was he trying to get me to tell him what he wanted to know? Maybe he thought I was chasing women or maybe he couldn't bring himself to say the word 'gay.'

'Well, I don't see how I can stop something when I don't know what it is I'm supposed to be stopping.'

'Don't get smart with me. And I'm not the only one who's onto you, so you'd better watch out.'

I looked him straight in the eye.

'Will that be all?'

He glared back at me but couldn't find the words to make a suitable response.

'And make sure you get replacements for those advertising blocks before the end of the month.'

I turned to walk away but couldn't resist one last swipe.

'It's nice to know you're so concerned about my misfortune.'

* * *

Henry had thrown down the gauntlet and I had picked it

up. As much as it unnerved me to live and work side by side with Henry, I was relieved that the burgeoning bubble of discontent between us had finally burst. After this, Henry seemed to make sure I was out of Bombay as often and for as long as possible. It turned out to be an acceptable solution for me, since gay friends in Bombay had been supplying me with contacts around the country and I couldn't wait to check them out. Moreover, it meant I could talk to colleagues who might have a little more distance on Henry.

So I was delighted when Henry declared that the following month I was to go with Kavita to Delhi for a week, then travel alone to Calcutta to work for the next two weeks before returning to Bombay. The journey to Delhi went without a hitch. Having an Indian colleague accompany me was a boon. We could keep an eye on each other's luggage, discuss things we would never talk about at home, and weather the storms of departure and arrival in a more relaxed fashion. I had known Kavita since my early days in India. A young mother of three, she was used to handling multiple demands but enjoyed being able to relinquish that responsibility from time to time. She cut a striking figure in her green and gold sari, with a red bindi between her eyebrows and the vermilion streak above her forehead. Her ability to switch back and forth between English and Hindi encouraged me to try the same. She would laugh at my attempts to direct taxi drivers and rickshaw-wallahs and wasn't averse to correcting my mistakes. Occasionally, she'd surprise me with a flirtatious comment, but I had an odd feeling she felt comfortable doing this with me.

During my week in Delhi, we had a full schedule of

appointments so I kept my personal activities to a minimum. I made sure my absences were not too conspicuous, especially with Tarabai hovering in the background. When we had to part company I was sorry to leave Kavita, but I was ready for time to myself that the overnight train journey to Calcutta would provide.

About 10 minutes before the Allahabad Express departed New Delhi station, a foreign woman appeared in the doorway of my compartment. In her early twenties and dressed in a maroon-flecked cotton dress that extended below her knees, she burst in on our all-male group with her brazen, youthful presence. Oh no, I thought. The last thing I wanted then was to make conversation with another foreigner.

'Is C-35 in here?' she asked, looking straight at me.

'Er, yes, I think so,' I replied.

I then noticed that seat space was occupied by a large man wearing a white dhoti.

'Excuse me, sir, but I think you are in the young lady's seat. Would you mind moving along a bit?'

He glowered at the latecomer then begrudgingly shuffled over slightly. Our new arrival wasted no time claiming what she regarded as rightfully hers.

'Hi. I'm Mitzy,' she said with an American accent.

'I'm John,' I replied, trying not to show my displeasure.

She ignored the other passengers and proceeded to chat with me.

'Where are you heading?' she inquired.

'Calcutta.'

'Me too!' she cried, as though I had hit the jackpot.

'Just my bloody luck,' I thought.

I glanced up and caught the kurta-clad man in the corner opposite casting a lascivious look in her direction. One quick flash of his eye was enough to tell me that he shared the widespread belief among Indian men that all young foreign women were fair game for their sexual advances.

As she was about to resume speaking, the sound of glass hitting metal rang out, followed by 'Thanda, thanda!' A boy lugging a heavy bucket stood at the opening of our compartment and chimed 'Limca, Thums Up.'

Without hesitating, Mitzy turned to me. 'Would you like a drink? My treat.'

This was one of those questions to which 'yes' was the only possible answer. We'd hardly spoken to each other and here she was buying me a drink. Americans can be very forward, I thought. Not as circumspect as Europeans or as reticent as Australians. As we downed our cold drinks, she again seized the initiative.

'So what are you doing in India?'

'I'm with an international voluntary organization doing a village development project.'

'What kind of development?'

'We introduce villagers to a community decision-making process and help them come up with a blueprint for their future.'

'That's cool.'

I flinched as she uttered the word. It was such a vacuous cliché that I vowed never to use it.

'How about you?' I asked.

'Oh, just bummin' around. But I managed to land a job in Delhi on a film shoot for a foreign movie.'

'Which film?'

'*The Far Pavilions*. Do you know it?'

'Sure do. It's one of my favorite books. I bought it in London a couple of years ago and read it on the plane coming here. What exactly did you do?'

'Nothing much. I was a wardrobe assistant and an extra in some of the crowd scenes.'

'Did you get to know any of the cast?'

'A little. The lead actors kept to themselves most of the time. I got to know one guy pretty well, though. He had his own car and driver. I really thought he liked me but it wasn't quite like that.'

'What do you mean?'

She began to shuffle her feet and turned towards me.

'Let's go out into the corridor. It's stuffy in here.'

Before I had a chance to answer, she stood up and headed to the open door and I followed. She leaned against the window and looked me in the eyes.

'The guy asked me to have dinner with him and even invited me to his trailer a couple of times. Then, one day one of the security men found him having sex with his driver in his car. Can you believe it? Indian men!'

I nearly dropped my Thums Up. Her revulsion at the thought of two men delighting in each other's bodies caught me off guard. My imagination shot into overdrive as I drifted off to another place.

'Excuse me,' she said. 'I hope I didn't offend you by what I said.'

'No, not at all,' I replied. 'I've heard that a lot of guys have sex with other men in India. They're not necessarily gay. You must have seen them walking around holding hands.'

'Weird if you ask me. Anyway, I've had enough of Indian men.'

How could I tell her I couldn't get enough of them? Her last sentence hung there like a barrier between us, its implications yet to sink in.

As the train raced eastwards, the numbing afternoon heat ebbed away into early evening. While the other members of our compartment read or dozed, Mitzy tried valiantly to engage me in conversation. Eventually she wore me down and I told her I needed to take a nap. Pretending to be asleep, I stretched out my legs and let my head droop to one side. At one point, I was sure I felt Mitzy pushing against my leg in rhythm with the sway of the train. I gently repositioned my leg and pretended not to notice.

Next morning, as we approached Howrah station, I looked forward to parting company. But it soon became apparent that extricating myself from Mitzy's clutches might not be quite so simple.

'Where are you staying in Calcutta?' she asked.

I told her about the crowded little house in a bustee alley that our staff rented.

'Sounds fascinating,' she said.

'How about you?'

'I'm checking into the Salvation Army hostel. Not quite the Grand you know, but it suits my budget.'

I knew we had to go close by the hostel in order to get to the bustee. I also knew how taxi drivers could rip off gullible foreigners, especially young women. So, as much as I wanted to be rid of Mitzy, I weakened and asked if she would like to share a taxi.

'I'd really appreciate that, being my first time in Calcutta and all. Thanks a lot.'

As she alighted from the cab, she took out a purse from her backpack and offered me 10 rupees. At the same time, she pulled out a notebook and ripped out a page.

'Why don't you write down your phone number and address?'

Like a dog chewing its favorite bone, she was not about to let me go. I was going to tell her we didn't have a phone, but knowing how unreliable Calcutta phones were, her chances of getting through were negligible. I scribbled down our number and address and gave it to her.

'Thanks,' she said. 'Been great to meet you. Hope to see you again. Take care.'

She picked up her backpack and headed for the hostel.

* * *

Monday night was 'family night' in our tightly ordered community life and since several foreigners were visiting our Calcutta office, we decided to all go out for dinner. Just as we were about to leave, the phone rang. It was Mitzy, asking if I would care to join her for dinner.

Since dropping her off at the hostel the morning before, I had shut Mitzy out of my mind. I told her I was about to go out with my colleagues, thinking this would terminate our conversation.

'Mind if I join you?' she asked.

'Well, er, no, of course not. But you'll have to get over here right away because we're about to leave.'

'Cool. Give me 15 minutes.'

Mitzy arrived just as we were still trying to find a taxi and introduced herself to my colleagues. I had explained to them how we'd met on the train but my words were met with a skeptical stare. She quickly ingratiated herself into our group, as we headed off to the leather tannery district, where I hoped to find a Chinese restaurant recommended to me by another train traveler. It was a huge gamble, but it paid off. After a hearty meal and lots of premium Calcutta beer, I was sure we were in for a hefty bill, but our Chinese host was adamant we were his guests and would accept no payment. The old Indian adage, 'the guest is a god,' seemed alive and well.

The night's drama didn't end when the taxi deposited us back in our bustee. Before I had the presence of mind to retain it, the taxi vanished into the darkness. Given how late it was, I felt obliged to accompany Mitzy back to her hostel. She insisted we take a rickshaw, something I'd vowed I would never do. But Mitzy was unrelenting, and given our options at this time of night, I caved in to her persistence.

As we bumped along in this flimsy contraption, our bodies rubbed against each other every time we hit a pothole or rattled over one of Calcutta's ubiquitous tram tracks. When we pulled up outside the hostel I paid the driver substantially more than we had agreed, as if to assuage my guilt. As I was figuring out my parting line, Mitzy upstaged me.

'Like to come in and see where I'm staying?'

'Thanks, but I'd better be going.'

'I have some imported Scotch.'

She wasn't letting 'no' get in the way of her agenda.

'I'm not much into whisky, especially after all that beer we had tonight,' I said.

'You know, I really appreciate what you did for me on the

train and inviting me out tonight. Sure you won't come up, even for a short while?'

I had one last card to play—my gay card. My mind tried to envision her possible responses if I did so. She might be offended I'd left it so long to mention it; she might feel I'd intentionally misled her and made her look a fool; she might get angry and make a scene. Then again, she might be apologetic and make me feel an idiot for holding back so long.

I decided not to risk discovering the answer and, in desperation, repeated my desire to return home. Grudgingly, she backed down and accepted that I was not going to join her. The look on her face was a cross between bewilderment and disgust. I had the distinct feeling I'd been lumped into the same subhuman category into which she had earlier discarded Indian men—either predatory beasts or wretched homosexuals. I probably deserved her wrath, but I vowed there and then I couldn't go on like this. It was time to come out to people, primarily those closest to me whom I trusted and respected. But who and when and how?

***

Life has an uncanny way of answering your questions, and it was a Friday night at the US Marines Club in Calcutta that it chose to answer mine. By the time we arrived, 'Thank God It's Friday' was in full swing. Sean and his American buddy made straight for the dart board, leaving Sandy and me to ourselves. The routines of community life and the intimate nature of our quarters didn't lend themselves to private discussions, so when a chance presented itself we usually didn't let it pass. Sandy reveled in such occasions.

I went to the bar to grab a couple of beers while Sandy claimed the one empty table in a quiet corner behind a potted palm. When I returned with our Heinekens, she looked me straight in the eye, shot me her toothy smile, and uttered what sounded like a well-rehearsed line.

'You know, John, Sean and I have been puzzled by you, especially your comings and goings at night. We've talked about it a lot and decided you either work for the CIA or you're gay. So which is it?'

Her candor caught me off guard. I looked at the palm tree, as if that would put words in my mouth, but as gracious as they are there are limits to what palms will do for you. Then, from somewhere within a voice said: 'Go on. This is the conversation you've been dying to have. Don't let it pass you by.'

Sandy could tell I was taken aback by her question and didn't know how to respond. She leaned over, took my hand, and said, 'It's okay, you can trust me. Honestly. Tell me all about it.'

The floodgates opened and out poured the story of my undulating journey of discovery over the last two years. Some episodes I thought better not to reveal, and others I played down. I suspected there would be time later for more details. But I privately rejoiced in having at last found someone in whom I could confide. How lucky I was that this someone was so sympathetic and understanding.

As we talked, Sandy revealed that she had several gay and lesbian friends. She and Sean had spent a couple of weeks the previous August in the UK with her former boyfriend and his partner. She assured me that Sean had no issue with my being gay. My sexual orientation was my own affair and another manifestation of the uniqueness of the individuals who were part of their team. For the first time, my divergent worlds began to edge a little closer.

* * *

On my return to Bombay, I was surprised to find an aerogramme from a friend in Australia whom I hadn't had contact with for several years. Graham and I went back to teenage days and our church youth group. Heavyset, with receding black hair and dark-rimmed glasses, he had been shy and diffident the first time we had met. His Anglo-Australian working-class accent made me wonder if he was fresh off the boat. Since the rest of us were about to head off to a coffee shop, I had asked him if he'd like to join us. Years later, he would remind me of that first meeting with a deep sense of gratitude. I was the only person who had made contact with him the whole evening.

Over the next few years, Graham and I rubbed shoulders off and on but found ourselves on separate tracks. I headed to university, while he had an assortment of jobs, before taking a course in culinary arts at a technology institute. I lost track of him until this letter mysteriously appeared in my mailbox. I opened it with a sense of intrigue. He had left Perth, joined the Institute in Sydney, and taken an assignment in Kenya with another village development project. He was leaving in a few weeks and would have stopovers in Singapore and Bombay. Would I be able to meet him and show him around? Fortunately, I happened to be in Bombay that week, so I gladly agreed. I also asked if he would buy me a replacement radio in Singapore, known for its cheap prices on electronic goods. His visit seemed fortuitous.

Graham's arrival came at a time when we had a full house, but he had no problem sleeping on the roof, which some of us occasionally did during Bombay's insufferable nights. The whole week Graham was with us I struggled with whether and how to tell him about my sexuality. Now that I had talked with Sandy, I was bursting to tell others too, but could I trust Graham with my secret? As the days slid by, the question grew in intensity.

During his brief stay, I wanted to give Graham the opportunity to contribute something to our community, as guests often did. Believing in his self-proclaimed reputation as a chef, I suggested we ask him to prepare an Australian-themed meal for our weekly roundtable, which was met with agreement. We settled on shepherd's pie. Obtaining one of the key ingredients—keema or minced lamb—was a lesson in local culture Graham never forgot.

The day of the dinner, I led him downstairs and into Sankli Street. As we turned left at the gate, Charlie greeted us by waving his stump furiously in our direction, so I introduced Graham to him.

'Mera dost Graham sahib, Australia se,' I said.

Graham wasn't sure how to respond but just as he was about to shower Charlie with a broad 'G'day,' I whispered in Graham's ear.

'Namastaiy,' he said, stretching out the final vowel as only an Australian can.

'Namaste,' responded Charlie, waving his head enthusiastically from side to side.

I explained our shopping expedition and Charlie gave us

his blessing as we headed in the direction of the butcher shops in the Muslim quarter.

Whenever I came down this way I made a point of stopping at my favorite juice stand and downing a glass of mango or guava. As much as I loved fresh fruit juice, it was the smart young man behind the counter who really slaked my thirst. His trim body and welcoming smile never failed to push my fantasy button. This day I decided to share my little fetish with Graham, without disclosing my hidden agenda. Between sipping drinks, I'd swear I caught him eyeing the juice-wallah.

After lingering as long as I could over our drinks, I slipped the juice-wallah an extra few rupees with my payment. The twinkle in his eye as he pocketed the money made it seem worth every paisa. Who knows what else he sold? A year ago, I wouldn't have entertained the thought, but now I had begun to see potential sexual partners everywhere. I found young, working-class men particularly appealing. Was it their lack of pretence, absence of intellectual hang-ups, or sheer pragmatism when it came to sex?

As we walked out of the shop, Graham surprised me by saying, 'Nice bloke, that juice guy.'

I nodded in agreement and pointed the way to the butcher's alley. Flies skittered around sides of mutton hanging on hooks and rivulets of blood ran in roadside drains. Graham grabbed my arm.

'This is where you buy meat?'

'Sure is.'

'You can't be serious. You could die eating this stuff.'

'Listen mate, there are so many ways you can die in India this one hardly rates.'

The meal went well, although I had second thoughts about having billed it as fine example of Australian cuisine. After dinner, I suggested we go downtown and check out a few places. Graham had gone off on his own during the day while I was working, but tonight was his last in Bombay, so it would be criminal not to go out together. We hopped in a taxi and headed for one of the city's best known landmarks, the Gateway of India, adjacent to the Taj Palace Hotel. Built to commemorate the visit of King George V and Queen Mary to India, it was now overrun by hawkers and snake charmers, buskers and sex-workers.

As soon as we arrived, I was surprised to run into a group of friends from the Bandstand. I had decided to bypass this regular hangout to avoid any awkward scenes, but I hadn't counted on this. Akbar, a tall, sharp-featured guy dressed in a finely pressed kurta, noticed me getting out of the taxi and came towards me. I introduced Graham to him and he led us over to his companions. Not sure of Graham's interests, they deftly skirted around the subject of sex, while their eyes darted here and there to see who they could pick among the crowd. I wasn't sure how long we could keep up this façade, so I bid them farewell and took Graham for a walk along the seawall before heading to the hotel for coffee. It wasn't until the next day I realized how much I had underestimated my Australian friend.

Unlike me, Graham had resources of his own, and so he wasn't at the mercy of our stipend system. I knew Graham had a generous streak, so I wasn't surprised when he insisted on taking me out for lunch at the revolving restaurant on top of the Ambassador Hotel before he left for the airport. After our third glass of beer and second plate of frog's legs in garlic sauce, I realized Graham had an agenda and intended to stick to it. He kept dragging up stories about our past and plying me with questions about my life. Did I have any plans to get married? Was I making out with any women? What did I do for fun these days? The more he pushed and probed, the more I sensed him trying to get closer to the truth. I decided to take the plunge.

'Well Graham, since you seem to be keen to know all about me, there is something I want to tell you that I've only told two other people. I'm gay.'

'I knew it!' he said, banging his fist on the table.

I had to grab my beer glass to stop it falling over.

'If only you'd told me when we went out on the town that night in Sydney, I would have taken you to some quite different places mate!'

My mind flashed back to a September night two years before. It was close to my birthday, and Graham was living in Sydney at the time. He insisted on taking me to one of the city's finest hotels for dinner, then on to King's Cross and several strip clubs. By 2.30 in the morning, I could barely stand up and made my way home, leaving Graham to his own devices. If only I'd known about myself at that time. Then somewhere in my brain a connection occurred.

'So you're gay too, are you?' I asked.

'Takes one to know one.'

At that, I picked up my glass and he followed suit.

'Cheers mate. Now we really have something to celebrate.'

As I mouthed the words, my eyes moistened. I couldn't believe it. First Sandy and now Graham, both within a couple of weeks. I felt as if a huge weight had been lifted from my shoulders. After two years of floundering to uncover who I was, I had finally found two people who seemed to understand what drove me to take such risks and who affirmed me for doing so. Within a short time, I would come to know of others—an entire network I never knew existed.

* * *

Unknown to me, since that evening at the Marines Club, Sandy had been sleuthing behind the scenes and had discovered another staff member in Chicago who was gay. Unlike me, he had been out to himself and certain members of the organization for some years but I had never heard of him. As soon as Sandy told me, I dashed off a letter to him. I could hardly believe it—another gay colleague. I had naively assumed that I was one of a kind in our organization. How had he managed to deal with his sexuality and stay part of the Institute? Did he know of others who were gay? Did they communicate with one another? I had oodles of questions to ask, apart from my own story to tell, so I wrote a long letter and asked a colleague returning to Chicago to act as courier to make sure it arrived safely.

In the meantime, I couldn't wait to continue my conversations with Sandy. Her willingness to listen and her unconditional acceptance of my being gay overwhelmed me. Moreover, she came across as genuinely concerned about my well-being. Her natural inquisitiveness and bubbly style endeared her to many. She could coax information out of a mute and seemed to delight in doing so. Yet I never had the impression she did this out of any puerile motives.

Opportunities to visit Calcutta increased in the first few months of 1983. In May, when the marriage season was in full swing and the mercury was on a steady rise, I spent three weeks in the city. As much as I longed to stay, this time I couldn't wait to return to Bombay to see if there might be a reply to my letter.

As soon as I arrived, I went straight to the mailboxes and collected the sheaf of letters awaiting me. The amount of correspondence bordered on embarrassing, most of it the light blue 'inland' letters. When someone remarked that I received a lot more mail than anyone else, I wondered how many others had also noticed and what questions it might have raised. I dreaded the possibility that one day someone might let curiosity get the better of them and open my mail in my absence.

I grabbed my bundle of letters, sat down in the office, and sorted through it. Most could wait until morning, but one could not. It was handwritten and postmarked Chicago. I stared at the sender's name. It was not from Jack, the person I had written to, but from another colleague named Barry, whom I had vaguely heard of. I tore it open and read it half aloud, so as not to miss a single word.

He began with an apology for having read a letter not addressed to him but explained that he and Jack were close friends and since Jack was on assignment in Central America, he was collecting his mail and thought I might wonder why I didn't hear back from him. Furthermore, a colleague in Bombay had written to another friend of theirs in Chicago, Elena, tipping her off that I was gay and asking her advice on how to deal with my situation. Elena had passed on the news to Barry, so when he saw my name on the envelope he felt compelled to open the letter.

At first I thought it strange that I should write a confidential letter to one person and receive a reply from another. But the more Barry explained who he was, his relationship with Jack and Elena, and conversations they had been having as gay members of the organization, the more grateful I was that he had seized the initiative to respond. I was stunned to discover there were others grappling with the same questions I was. They were delighted to find another colleague half a world away and in a vastly different cultural milieu, whom they could welcome to join them. It had the feel of a secret cadre within the party ranks.

I sat in the sweltering stillness, staring at the letter in my hand. Outside, the raging traffic had subsided to a trickle, with an occasional tinkle of a bicycle bell and blast of a taxi horn. I turned off the light and pondered the synchronicity of it all. Was it merely chance that a little over two years ago I had picked up that sexology magazine? Was it happenstance that I decided one Sunday afternoon to head down to Chowpatty Beach? Were the beatings and muggings I had endured trials sent to test my decision? And what of my confrontation with Henry, that brought my two worlds clashing together? I felt as though I only had to take that initial step, then let some mysterious force lead me onward. Although my destination was far from clear, I knew I was on a journey that could redefine my life. There was a sense of urgency about that journey, for at 33 years of age I felt like an athlete in a long-distance race, lagging far behind the leaders with a lot of ground to make up.

Now that I had revealed my hand, I began to find new momentum. As soon as Jack returned to Chicago and read my letter, he wrote straight back. His fluent handwriting and upbeat style suggested someone who knew what he wanted out of life and was determined to get it. As I eagerly read his letter, I was enthralled by his story. Since his undergraduate days in Minnesota, he had been connected with the Institute and often visited its neighborhood project in the Chicago ghetto. After three years as a Peace Corps volunteer in El Salvador, he had joined the Institute in Minneapolis, whose leaders understood he was gay. They treated him with respect and gave him major program responsibilities, while he continued to lead an active gay life outside the community. Given that this was the mid-1970s and that questions of sexual orientation were rarely discussed, his was a bold move. It would be another decade before such questions would be forced out into the open within the organization.

But Jack's experiences weren't always so positive. When reassigned to another location in a more conservative part of the country, its fundamentalist Southern Baptist director stated publicly one day that he was kicking Jack out because he was a goddamn queer. Being fluent in Spanish, Jack soon found his services in demand in the Institute's emerging development projects in South America. His amiable and energetic style won him many friends among villagers and staff alike, but local mores and a strong Latino macho tradition demanded he put his sexual life on hold—at least while in the village. Cities were another matter, with temptations and dangers of their own.

From his experience with the Institute over a number of

years, Jack had come to several conclusions. With the one exception, he had never been mistreated by people who knew he was gay, but it was patently clear that the subject was off limits. No one ever talked to him about it or asked what he thought about it in relation to the goals and values of the organization. He always suspected that the Institute's tolerance of his homosexuality was contingent on him conducting that part of his life outside its sphere of influence. Within the community, it was assumed he had to be asexual. Moreover, in public meetings he had had to endure homophobic remarks and anti-gay jokes, while those who knew he was gay remained silent.

Jack predicted it would be many years before the Institute would take an affirmative stance towards homosexuality, and he wasn't willing to wait that long. He wrote, 'I will be 36 next month and am not looking forward to living a single life much longer … Staying around and helping in the healing process is a price I'm not willing to pay.' I was both proud of his stance and saddened by his decision. Meanwhile, Jack, Barry and Elena had discussed my situation and were convinced I must come to Chicago in July for our annual global leadership meeting, with the expectation that I would be reassigned there afterwards. They planned to present the issue of gay and lesbian participation in the organization at a major staff gathering in Chicago the following year, and wanted me to work with them on it.

Their request sent me into a tailspin. While I was excited at the prospect of being a part of this new and groundbreaking proposal, the thought of leaving India in six weeks seemed preposterous. I was not ready for it. Preparations for the exposition were surging ahead and I was intimately involved in many of the details. I couldn't conceive not being in India when the event unfolded the following February. But most of all, I didn't feel ready to abandon the many gay friends I had acquired. I still had much more exploring to do. I was a slow starter but a strong finisher and in my journey of sexual discovery I was nowhere near the finish line yet. Over the next few weeks, letters from Jack, Barry and Elena filled my mailbox, each begging me to join them in 'the Lavender League.' Barry was a member of a group working on staff assignments and could arrange my transfer. I only had to say yes.

But I could not bring myself to do so. 'I'll cry if I have to leave here, I'm so attached,' I wrote in a letter to a friend. 'India is a very, very human society. Relationships are key and people are so responsive.' What's more, I had become so enamored with Indian men that other nationalities didn't interest me. It took years before this changed; in some ways it never did. Feeling like a traitor to the cause, I resolved to stay in India. When a packet of articles arrived from Barry, along with an imploring letter, I was tempted to give in to his pressure. Instead, I came up with a compromise plan, that had me arriving in Chicago the following January, after stopovers in Australia to visit my mother and in New Zealand to see Jeremy. Jack's first letter to me had raised serious questions about whether I wanted to stay with the Institute as a gay man, or follow his lead and quit. I needed people both inside and outside the organization with whom I could talk this through.

As it turned out, none of my plans eventuated. The next 12 months in India would prove to be the most challenging but most rewarding yet.

FLYING HIGH

People were beginning to fidget in their chairs. It was 4.10 pm and still no sign of Sir James. You don't keep CEOs waiting like this. I glanced at my watch and then at my colleagues. 'Where on earth could he be?' was the question on every face in the room.

At 4.15 pm, the sound of approaching footsteps made all eyes turn towards the door. In burst Sir James and his entourage. He looked wiped out, sweat trickling down his brow onto his brown jacket. After several appointments and a working lunch already that day, he was in no shape to address this distinguished gathering of the upper crust of Bombay's business fraternity.

Trying to assume some measure of composure, Sir James glanced up as his host began introducing him from the podium. It was no secret to the audience that he was still frantically trying to arrange his notes for his speech. Well accustomed to the protocol of such occasions, Sir James arose as if on cue to deliver his talk.

As he made to stand, his left hand strayed off course and

collided with the microphone, which fell to the floor. Never one to rely on others for help, Sir James plunged in pursuit of the apparatus. As he did so, he lost control of his notes and found himself on the floor amid a sea of paper.

'Excuse me, ladies and gentlemen,' said a beleaguered voice from below. 'I'll be with you in a minute.'

This comment brought a chuckle or two from the audience, some of whom were beginning to see the humor in the situation. Others seemed to be saying 'My god, who is this person?' After a couple of minutes, Sir James righted himself and attempted to begin once more.

'Pardon me,' he said in his most polite English voice, 'but I have misplaced page one. I shall have to ad lib a little, if you don't mind.'

No one seemed to. They were just glad the show was finally getting on the road.

This memorable afternoon at the Taj Palace Hotel in Bombay was my introduction to Sir James. Intelligent and personable, he had joined a well-known package and container fabrication company in UK and soon found himself transferred to their India operations, headquartered in Calcutta, where he rose swiftly through the ranks. During his time in India, the company grew from two plants and 1,400 employees to 10 plants and 10,000 employees. As Calcutta continued to bask in the fading light of its former glory as the capital of British India, entitled expatriates seemed to occupy a world unto themselves. This was the world Sir James was part of—he belonged to the right clubs, swam at the Gymkhana pool, and ate at fashionable restaurants as befitted the life of a Calcutta boxwallah. But he shunned the pretentiousness and exclusivity that so often accompanied this way of life. For more than 30 years, he had called the city home. He had spent 16 of those years living in the spacious house his company provided for its top executive in the highly desirable suburb of Alipore. He had married three times—in two instances after having broken taboos by crossing the racial divide.

But it wasn't only in matters of the heart that he was a social pioneer. Having stayed on after Independence in 1947, he had led the way in bringing Indian managers into the top rungs of his company. He was the founding president and a life member of the All-India Management Association and had made sure he was the last British president of that august body. In 1964, during a time of high tension between India and Pakistan, a senior British cabinet minister had accused India of instigating the conflict. His comments threatened to damage relations between India and Britain, and business relationships in particular. Enter Sir James. Over a two-month period, his intensive efforts at shuttle diplomacy, involving frequent trips to the UK, not only helped defuse the crisis but also earned him a knighthood for his services. It was a role for which he was most suited with his peculiar blend of courage, sensitivity, and a nose for diplomatic nuance.

Leaving India must have been a wrenching moment in Sir James' life, but when the time came in 1969 he returned to the UK where he remarried and took up a teaching position at the distinguished Henley Management College. This college attracted students from all over the world, mostly the crème de la crème from different countries, many of them newly independent nations like India. Hundreds of them passed through Sir James' capable hands and returned home to become prominent leaders of business, industry and government. During his tenure at Henley, Sir James was contacted by the Institute's London staff about a strategic planning seminar. He was intrigued by the approach and sought to learn more about the organization, especially its work in India. When the idea of the exposition was mooted, we knew it would take someone with global connections and a keen understanding of India to help us win support and funding for the project. We asked Sir James if he would be willing to play such a role. To our delight he accepted, and propelled the Institute to new levels of power and influence in many countries. Like me, the organization found it had a lot of growing up to do, and fast.

From the moment I first met him, I was charmed by the man. The more I worked with him, the more I learned to appreciate the depth and intensity of his character. His incredible memory for detail, his indefatigable pace of work, his respect for people of all rank and class, his ability to operate in a variety of cultures, his wide-ranging language skills—I heard him speak Hindi, Bengali, French, Spanish, Bahasa Indonesian, and Japanese—were some of his many impressive qualities. But most of all, it was his unapologetic humanity that left an indelible mark on me.

In the years leading up to the exposition, Sir James became the Institute's public face to the world and we worked him and his wife to the bone. They were constantly criss-crossing the globe to cement authorization and solicit funding for the exposition. During this time, I had the pleasure of working with him in India, as well as in other parts of Asia. On one occasion, we were on a flight together from Tokyo to Hong Kong. When we left Tokyo, it had been five degrees Celsius.

As the plane landed in Hong Kong, the captain announced that it was 28 degrees outside. Anticipating the dramatic climate change, Sir James suddenly stood in the middle of the plane and started to change his clothes.

'Jim, what *are* you doing?' asked his wife in disbelief.

'Well, you heard what the captain said, didn't you? Twenty-eight bloody degrees out there and I'm rugged up like I'm about to climb the Himalayas.'

'Yes, but you can't change in the middle of a plane.'

'I don't see why not,' he quipped. 'They do it on the beach, don't they?'

Sensing she was fighting a losing battle, his wife proceeded to exit with the other passengers, while I looked the other way and waited for Sir James to complete his change of costume, seemingly oblivious to the lines of people shuffling down the aisles and gazing in open-mouthed wonder.

Being exposed to the private Sir James as well as his public persona was a double thrill for me. The former didn't detract from the latter; it only enhanced it. It was easy to understand why the memory of him lingered long after he had left India, among both the top echelons of society and those much lower on the ladder. This was underscored for me the night I accompanied him to dinner at Bombay's exclusive Willingdon Club, as guests of the chairman of one of India's leading food manufacturing companies. Once the enclave of the British imperial establishment, the Willingdon was now firmly in the hands of wealthy Indians. We had barely seated ourselves at the circular table when the chief waiter, adorned in elaborate head gear and a trailing saffron sash, recognized Sir James. He rushed up to him, bowed low, and touched his feet while uttering profuse greetings. I'm certain I noticed Sir James' eyes moisten as he graciously acknowledged the honor he had been paid. He then turned to his host and said, 'I feel awful but I can't remember that gentleman's name.'

Sir James' connections with so many of India's economic and political leaders were like a golden key that magically opened door after door. While we had assiduously courted government and business leaders in support of our own village projects, doing so for an international event of the magnitude we were planning was a wholly different matter. We were being forced to metamorphose from a little-known NGO to a sophisticated international body that walked with kings and princes. We had to acquire a new level of professional acumen appropriate to our role, while continuing our regular work. We began receiving phone calls from private secretaries of people we would never have had the remotest chance of seeing, had it not been for Sir James. Members of our staff would accompany him on visits and I was fortunate to be chosen to play this role on several occasions.

One that stands out took place within walking distance of our humble staff quarters in the Calcutta bustee. Sandy and I decided to walk to save a taxi fare and join Sir James and his wife at the appointment. It was a bright, clear Sunday morning and as we strolled along the luscious scent of frangipani overpowered us. I was wearing my newly dry-cleaned safari suit and Sandy had on a white cotton dress with dark blue spots. We had decided to allow plenty of time in case we should have difficulty locating the house. But No. 18 Gurusaday Dutta Road was hard to miss, since it occupied most of a block. Its waist-high concrete fence bordered a huge expanse of lawn and tropical plants behind which sprawled the residence of Mr. and Mrs. B K Birla.

Basant Kumar Birla was the grandson of Baldeo Das Birla, a Marwari from Rajasthan who had moved to Calcutta in the late 19th century to set up the family business. Today, the Birla empire includes dozens of companies from petrochemicals to textiles, automobiles to information systems. The Birlas are also known for their participation in India's freedom movement. Mahatma Gandhi was once their house guest in Delhi. Little wonder, then, that it was with a sense of awe and trepidation that Sandy and I approached the guard at the Birla's front gate. I whipped out my business card, making sure I dropped the name of Sir James as I did so. The guard stared at the card, then at us, and back at the card.

'You wait here,' he commanded, and raced off down the drive at a rapid pace.

Sandy and I looked at each other, mystified. The Birlas knew Sir James was coming, so surely they had alerted the gateman. Within minutes, voices emanated from the porch at the entrance to the house. One of them was that of an older woman. The guard sprinted back to his post and beckoned us with his right hand.

'Sorry, very sorry,' he said as he ushered us in the slowly opening metal gate. 'Madam is awaiting you.'

When we reached the house, Mrs. Birla, wearing an exquisite blue and green silk sari, came down the steps to greet us. She apologized profusely for the misunderstanding. Sandy and I brushed it aside, but when she informed us she had been told there were a couple of hippies at the gate, we couldn't restrain our laughter.

While we were all still enjoying the joke, Sir James' car entered the driveway. He and his wife joined us on the steps just as Mr. Birla appeared at the door. As we walked through the entryway into the house, my eyes strained to stay in their sockets. It was as though we had been dropped into a museum and gallery of world cultures, generously endowed with items from the Subcontinent. I would later learn that their collection of ancient Indian sculptures, miniature paintings, bronzes, textiles and terracotta is regarded as a national treasure.

As the morning wore on and we talked further, it was Mrs. Birla who captured my attention more than her better-known husband. She modestly revealed that she played several classical Indian instruments and spoke a handful of foreign languages, as well as a number of Indian ones. What she didn't tell me was that in addition to her love of the visual arts, music, dancing and literature, she was a passionate promoter of education for young Indian women, which had led her to establish several private schools for girls. After more than an hour in her presence, I began to feel like a hippy. My efforts and those of our organization paled into insignificance compared to what she had accomplished. Granted she was 60 and I was scarcely half her age; granted she had been born into wealth and trained to use it to good effect. Nevertheless, I stood in awe of her. Living in a society in which women are so often relegated to secondary status, she had used her privilege, affluence and education to fight injustice and had something to show for her efforts. I began questioning what I had done with my life and came up short.

Two days later, when I stopped by the Birla office to pick up a check for 100,000 rupees for the exposition, I found myself in a state of renewed shock. It was the largest amount of money I had ever held in my hands and was a great boost to our fundraising campaign, practically and symbolically. But I had received riches of a far greater kind. The Birlas had shown me that a sense of compassion and social justice was not limited to indigenous social activists or foreign volunteers.

If the Birlas are one of India's two leading family-owned industrial empires, the other indisputably are the Tatas. A Parsi family based in Bombay, the Tatas are equally renowned for their wide-ranging commercial enterprises, comprising close on 100 companies in multiple sectors, from hotels and vehicles to tea and computer software. The Tata Group pioneered in many fields after India's independence and its contribution to the country's education, science and technology is widely acknowledged. One of the jewels in the Tata crown is the Tata Iron and Steel Company (TISCO), established in 1907 in Jamshedpur. For many years, its chairman and managing director was another Parsi, Russi Mody.

The son of a governor of West Bengal, Mody was educated at Oxford and became a legend in his own lifetime for the way he ran TISCO. He was gregarious and outgoing, noted for his sharp wit and personal charm, skills he put to good use in negotiating with union leaders and governments alike. He was highly popular in Calcutta, evidenced by the number of people, including many former employees, who would shower him with gifts and garlands each year on his birthday. It was hardly surprising that Sir James and he were known to each other, and in some ways they possessed similar qualities. To have Russi Mody's support for the exposition would be a sizable feather in our Indian cap. When he agreed to meet

Sir James, our Calcutta staff were thrilled. When he invited Sir James and his associates to lunch at his home, we were beside ourselves. When I was asked to accompany Sean and Sir James, I felt I had stepped out of reality into a movie.

Russi Mody owned three homes—one in London, one in Darjeeling in the foothills of the Himalayas, and a penthouse apartment atop the TISCO building in Calcutta overlooking the spacious maidan.Whereas the Birla residence stretched out, Mody's went up. As we ascended in the elevator, escaping the squalor and mayhem of street level, I imagined I was shedding part of myself and acquiring a new persona. I felt uneasy and out of place, and glad to have Sean for support. I decided my best strategy was to lie low and let Sir James follow his well-oiled routine.

When the elevator could go no further, we stepped out into the air-conditioned lobby and Sean rang the bell. Seconds ticked away. I moved my weight from one foot to the other. The door burst open to reveal a squat little man with a protruding waistline.

'Jim, old boy, how wonderful to see you after all these years!' exclaimed an exuberant Mody, extending his hand to welcome his guest.

Sir James reciprocated and after a suitable pause, introduced Sean and myself. As the two of them became reacquainted, I cast my eyes around the room. Much like the Birla mansion, the walls were covered with paintings, while art objects adorned the dustless cabinets and polished sideboards. But what captivated me more than anything else was a shining, black grand piano in the corner of the room. I knew Mody had many talents but I didn't know that piano playing was one of them. During a brief lull in the conversation, I asked him, 'That's a very fine Steinway grand you have there Mr. Mody. What kind of music do you play?'

'Quite a variety, actually. Some popular, some classical. You know, when I was a young student at Oxford, I accompanied Einstein on the piano while he played his violin. It was a lot of fun.'

How do you respond to a statement like that? Oh really, what did you play? Whose idea was it that you play together? How would you rate Einstein's musical talent? Every thought that flitted through my brain I banished instantly. I decided to sit out the rest of the meeting in silence. Sir James promptly picked up the ball and kept it bouncing, enumerating the names of other chums of his who had trod the hallowed halls of Oxford and who may have been contemporaries of Mody.

At another such meeting due to Sir James' influence and involvement, I found myself sitting across the desk and chatting with a future prime minister of India. Dr. Manmohan Singh was a man of humble beginnings, born in what is now Pakistan. He walked to school barefoot and studied under a street lamp because his house had no electricity. He went on to earn impressive degrees at Oxford and Cambridge before returning to India to take up academic posts and become a distinguished civil servant. One of the many prominent positions he held before becoming prime minister was that of Governor of the Reserve Bank of India. During this time, Sir James visited Bombay and while he was there we secured an appointment with his former acquaintance.

At first glance, the notion of visiting a government banking official didn't have the glitter and pizzazz that accompanied meetings with leading members of India's private sector, but it was an assignment I gladly accepted. Ensconced in the back of his chauffeur-driven Ambassador, Sir James and I made our way to the Reserve Bank building that soared high above the city's financial district. When our car dropped us at the building's entrance, one of Dr. Singh's aides met us and whisked us to the Governor's office on the top floor. Within minutes, we were ushered through teak-paneled doors into the inner sanctum of the nation's highest financial officer.

A middle-aged, genteel looking man dressed in a light grey Nehru suit stood up from behind his desk and walked towards us. Wearing a tightly wound blue turban and sporting a whitish beard, he gave the impression of someone who attended to detail with great finesse. But it was his eyes that struck me most. Framed by a pair of large-rimmed glasses, they contained a strange mixture of intelligent perception and calming warmth. I sensed I was in the presence of a man of considerable strength and vision but with a compassionate nature. As we sipped our tea and nibbled on cream biscuits, Sir James described the exposition and the Institute's role as organizing sponsor. He concluded his presentation with a request to his host to become a member of the exposition's Global Advisory Board. While this role required little more than allowing one's name to appear on promotional material, it was critical for gaining endorsement for the exposition. I was elated when Dr. Singh consented.

* * *

My encounters with Sir James didn't end in India. Several years later, we met in Brussels at the Institute's international headquarters, where I was then posted. Sir James was visiting and had a spare evening, so I asked if he would join me for dinner at a neighborhood restaurant. He welcomed the invitation and told me to come to his room at an agreed time. When I did, I found him in his underwear doing push-ups in the narrow space between bed and wall. He asked me to take a seat while he completed his regime, then proceeded to dress and polish his dark brown shoes with great zeal. When he finished, he turned to me and said, 'I don't suppose you could use this, could you?' Never one to turn down a gift, I gladly accepted his plastic, throw-away shoe polishing kit. I still have it, as a curious memento of many wonderful moments spent with Sir James.

We walked around the corner into Place St. Josse, where I suggested going to one of my favorite Italian restaurants. As we munched on lasagna and downed a glass of Chianti, we reminisced about India and the Institute. I kept looking for the opportune moment to steer the conversation in the direction I wanted it to go. Something told me that Sir James wouldn't give a fig about my sexual orientation, but because of my respect and fondness for the man I wished to share this news with him. I had learned from accompanying him in India that he never said no to dessert, so when I tempted him with a tiramisu, he jumped at the offer. I couldn't put it off any longer. I put my down my fork and cleared my throat.

'Sir James, there's something I've been meaning to mention to you for some time now. About myself, I mean. I don't know whether you've heard via the grapevine or guessed perhaps, but I'm gay. A late bloomer, too. It took India to help me come to terms with this part of myself.'

He didn't blink an eyelid but picked up his napkin and wiped some crumbs from his mouth.

'I didn't know that, but thank you for telling me,' he said reassuringly. 'I have a brother in Sydney who is homosexual. He's in the theater and a damn fine actor too.'

He pronounced 'homosexual' in the traditional British way with the first 'o' as in 'hot.' I asked him about his brother and he asked me about my experiences in India. I spoke frankly and he listened patiently, only occasionally butting in to ask a question.

'It sounds that you have rather catholic tastes, catholic with a small "c" that is.'

'That's a pretty accurate description,' I said, 'although since India it's been hard to extend my catholicism farther afield.'

He acknowledged my comment with a gleam in his eye. It was easy to imagine that his 32 years in India must have cast a similar spell over him, as my six years had on me, even though we were polar opposites in our sexual tastes. I was surprised at how easy it had been to share this part of my life with Sir James. It made me wonder what it would have been like to do the same with my father, had he been alive. Although I always considered my dad as a kind and thoughtful man, I doubt he had had the breadth of experience and exposure to the world that would have allowed him to accept my news with the same equanimity as Sir James. I would never know. But I was certain my mother would have considerably more difficulty coming to terms with it. Breaking the news to her called for careful planning on my part. A major step in this direction involved getting her to visit me in India, a scheme in which Sir James and his wife would play a critical role.

A TURN OF EVENTS

In Hindu mythology, the elephant-headed god Ganesh is known for many things, but mostly as the remover of obstacles.

A benevolent being, he is also worshipped as the harbinger of prosperity, well-being and wisdom. In Western India in particular, he has a strong and loyal following. Bombayites pour their passion into creating idols of their favorite deity, some so tiny they can be held in the palm of your hand, others so massive they have to be carried on the back of a truck. Months before the celebration known as Ganesh Chaturthi, artisans labor long into the night to perfect their creations. After 10 days of performing pujas to the pot-bellied god on family altars, devotees carry their beloved idols down every artery and vein of this labyrinthine city to the Arabian Sea for a farewell immersion. Crowds whip themselves into a frenzy with devotional singing and wild dancing to pulsating drumbeats and rattling tambourines.

I would usually try to avoid the parade route, but this year I wasn't so lucky. I had gone to visit a friend and on my way back became caught up in the procession. To add to the celebratory chaos in the streets, a storm had blown in off the Indian Ocean and deluged the city. In other parts of the world, such a torrential downpour may have dampened spirits, but not Bombay. If anything, it only buoyed the crowd into an even giddier mood. In an effort to escape the onslaught, I joined dozens of others who had taken shelter under a bus stand. Overflowing drains spewed foul water into the street, while a nearby billboard was ripped apart by blustering winds. The singers kept singing, the dancers kept dancing, and the parade went on, as if oblivious to the fury of the elements.

While I didn't overtly swear my allegiance to this benign being, I must have offered some propitiation by being part of the melee on that day because soon after, doors began to open in my life, almost before I had knocked on them. Not only doors into the homes and offices of the wealthy and powerful, but much lesser portals as well. Moreover, a major obstacle in my life was mysteriously removed, without any covert manipulation on my part. Two events bore testimony to this mysterious presence of Lord Ganesh in my life.

* * *

The first took place in Kolhapur District in south-western Maharashtra where I had worked several years before in one of our village projects. A bastion of the once-dominant Maratha empire, Kolhapur is known for its vast sugar factories, fine educational institutions, and thriving Marathi film industry, as much for its leather chappals, champion wrestlers, and spicy cuisine. It also boasted one of the highest per capita incomes in India, a resource I inadvertently tapped into when

I solicited the support of the city's many service clubs for our project. I made contact with all of them and developed a number of close friends—doctors, architects and businessmen among them. While these men and women were polite to my Indian colleagues, they always treated me with a special deference. Several families took a personal interest in my welfare, referring to me as their adopted son, an honor that touched me profoundly but which I learned later came with strings attached. When one family, gravely concerned about my status as a single man, began suggesting possible marriage partners, I found myself in an awkward situation. My apparent lack of interest in the subject puzzled and concerned them and introduced an awkward tension into an otherwise amicable relationship.

Now, several years later, I had returned to Kolhapur under different circumstances, professional and personal. No longer was I launching a village development project but raising money for the organization's work and the international exposition. No longer was I confused and ambivalent about my sexuality. I had tasted the fruit of the forbidden tree and I couldn't get enough of it. But how could I share with my Indian host families what was taking place in my life? I feared that news of my being gay would not only come to them as an incomprehensible mystery but also as a deep offence, in light of their unquestioned assumption that I, like a good son, would marry and produce offspring. As a consequence, I found myself telling lies and fabricating stories, skirting around the truth like an ice skater swerving in and out to avoid collisions.

In August 1983, I had a week to myself and decided to

revisit Kolhapur, but not with the intention of renewing old acquaintances. The reason for the visit had its roots six months before when I had gone there with Kavita on our annual fundraising drive. We had had a productive week and enjoyed being pampered as guests of one of my former adoptive families. But between work and socializing with our hosts, I had no time to pursue my own agenda. As a college town, Kolhapur had no shortage of good-looking young men, but sadly they remained out of reach. Walking around town was like being in a museum where you could look but not touch.

Towards the end of our stay, I had gone to the railway station to purchase our return tickets to Bombay. As I stood in line, I noticed a smart young man in the queue behind me but I didn't pay too much attention to him. Likewise, he didn't seem terribly interested in me, other than what I took to be the usual interest in a foreigner in a small regional city. Once I had obtained our tickets, I made straight for the men's toilet and was about to leave the urinal when the person I had eyed entered the room and came up to stand next to me. Unzipping his fly with great alacrity, he left me in no doubt as to his interest. Although it was early morning and few people were at the station, I was concerned that anyone could walk in unannounced, so I suggested we repair to a toilet stall and transact our business there. After we had done so, we shared addresses and phone numbers and parted company. We knew virtually nothing about each other, although he claimed to be a student named Gautam. I never expected to see him again.

However, once I returned to Bombay I began receiving numerous letters from Gautam embellished with adoring words and suggestive graphics. He begged me to return to Kolhapur at my earliest opportunity so we could pick up where we had left off. When the chance presented itself, I didn't hesitate and purchased a ticket for the overnight bus from Bombay. He had arranged for us to stay at a hill station west of Kolhapur for several days, which sounded blissful. We agreed to rendezvous at a local bus station from where we would travel together. I arrived at our meeting point in good time and positioned myself where I would easily be seen. Within a short time, Gautam showed up wearing brown trousers and a yellow T-shirt, along with chappals and dark sunglasses. I recognized him right away, even though he was dressed quite differently from when we last met.

But when he took off his glasses and looked me in the eye, the smiling face I was expecting to see was not there. Instead, I was confronted by a blank stare and a mouth turned down at the corners. When I offered my right hand, he countered with an unenthusiastic shake. I was dumbstruck. This was not the reception I was anticipating. Was this the same person who had written me all those suggestive letters? What on earth had happened to him?

On the two-hour bus journey to the hill station, I tried to elicit responses to those questions, but the more I probed, the more reticent Gautam became. Whatever was troubling him, he wasn't about to reveal it. Once we arrived at our destination, he was in no mood to engage in the kind of sexual fiesta I had envisaged. It was as much as I could do to keep words flowing between us. Despondently, I agreed to his suggestion that we return to Kolhapur and go our separate ways. As we shook hands for the last time, I felt disillusioned and abandoned.

What was most disturbing was that I couldn't fathom what I might have done to cause Gautam to act so strangely. Not knowing was harder than the rejection itself.

There were still five days left before I needed to be back in Bombay. I had no desire to return home, having invested the time and money to come all this way. I also had little interest in seeking solace from former friends. I could take a cheap hotel and try ferreting out places to meet other guys but my enthusiasm for this had waned markedly. I sat down in the bus station refreshment room and mulled over my options. Finally, I decided to get in touch with a family who had repeatedly asked me to stay with them but whose kind offer I'd never taken up. Their two sons, both married, lived with their families in the same extended household as their parents. The father and one of the sons, Sandip, were respected architects, as evidenced by their modern home. Its strategically placed windows illumined spacious rooms, tastefully decorated with bronze statues of Nataraja and images of the elephantine Ganesh. I called Sandip and his brother answered. He said that Sandip was at his other house in a village about four hours' drive west of Kolhapur. He was sure Sandip would be glad to have company, and suggested I join him there. I was delighted to accept, so he called the village post office to inform Sandip of my arrival.

The bus ride over potholed roads winding up the Ghats and down the other side transported me to a whole other India. The monsoon had arrived a few weeks earlier so everything was as clover green as an Irish landscape, but without the accompanying chill in the air. In an area that receives about 3,500 millimeters of rain a year, waterfalls materialized in the most surprising places, creating the impression that the countryside was one gigantic fountain with spouts scattered over the lush terrain. But the rain was not all benign. Frequent mudslides made the already dangerous road more risky. I found myself silently repeating the mantra I had come to use when traveling in India—trust the driver. These men who risked driving on roads that would test rally drivers had earned my respect. The further we drove, the more I became aware of the remoteness of villages in this region. Stops were few and usually at intersections from where a road wound endlessly to a village secreted far back in the mountains.

For the first time in India, I sensed I had stepped back from the maelstrom of life. As if having taken a deep breath I was gradually exhaling. The rough terrain made it impossible to read, so my mind fumbled around, looking for something to cling to, tossing out fragments of my life from the last two years to the last two days. Places, people, letters, questions, comments, ecstatic highs and repugnant lows all jostled for attention. Something told me it was time to step back from the brink and reflect on what had happened to me. This unexpected diversion, the fiasco with Gautam, my decision to return to Kolhapur—all of it began to fall into place like a jigsaw puzzle taking shape.

It was early evening when the red and yellow Tata bus rounded a bend and ground to a halt at Sandip's village. I may have arrived at my destination, but still needed to figure out how to find Sandip. I didn't have to wait long for help. Within seconds, a bevy of small boys descended on me. A foreigner coming to their village was clearly cause for great excitement.

'Hello. Tujhe naw kay ahe? What is your name? Kiti wazle? How are you? Tujhe desh ahe? What is your native place?' The familiar mish-mash of English and Marathi questions bombarded me from all sides. I was back in the real India, and like an actor responding to his cue, donned my public persona and assumed the character I was so used to performing—the enchanting foreigner, the honored guest, the curious outsider. Any notion of privacy and seclusion had vanished. As soon as I revealed I was from Australia, there were gasps from the back of the crowd, as the older boys recognized the name of this well-known cricketing country. I only had to mention Sandip's name and was beset with offers to lead me to him.

After leaving the main road, we cut through several small lanes and headed for a forest of majestic teak trees on the outskirts of the village. Just before we came to the towering canopy, we turned a sharp corner and came face to face with Sandip. At first I didn't quite recognize him in his traditional kurta and pajamas. The last time I had seen him he was wearing blue jeans and an open-neck shirt. As he approached me, the crowd dispersed and he held out his right hand.

'Ah, so you found me! What a pleasant surprise, John. I never thought you'd take up my offer to visit. Welcome to my other home.'

Sandip's other home turned out to be deceptively like many other village houses on the outside but closer examination revealed it had been designed by someone with well-honed architectural skills and an eye for simplicity and convenience. Although it contained a number of utilities of a modern, urban Indian home, it also had a Gandhian-like frugality. Well lit and well ventilated, it provided an enviable model for other villagers to follow. Sandip's housekeeper did not have to suffer the debilitating effects of cooking on a wood fire on a dung floor in a small hut with the door as the only exit for smoke. Nor did she have to wash clothes by pounding them against the rocks of the nearby stream. The moderately spiced vegetarian meals she prepared during my short stay were a welcome contrast to the usual stomach-torching dishes I had endured in my first stay in a Kolhapuri village.

I took an immediate liking to Sandip, which I sense was reciprocated. It was not a sexual attraction, which came as a strange kind of relief after all my philandering the last couple of years. It was more a meeting of kindred spirits and like-minded souls. He was a bright, successful and creative young man from a wealthy Indian family who valued his culture's traditions but was no prisoner to them. He was an innovator and adventurer in his work, while being a dutiful husband and father. He was as at home in the city as he was in this village. He straddled many worlds and appeared contented with his lot.

As soon as we reached his house, he had his housekeeper prepare chai and poha—the first of many teas we would share over the next few days and one I greatly appreciated after my long bus journey. As we sat on cushions on the wooden floor, Sandip looked me in the eye and asked, 'So, what would you like to do while you are here?'

I couldn't remember being asked such a question in a long time. It was like being given a blank check and all I had to do was fill in the amount. I paused as I sipped my chai and gathered my thoughts.

'Well, apart from enjoying some of the beautiful

surroundings in this lush part of the country, there is one thing I would like to do. It came to me on the way here today. I have been so busy working and having new experiences that I haven't taken the time to sort out what it all means and where it's leading me. I think I need to pause and reflect on what has happened to me these last couple of years in India. This strikes me as an ideal time and place to do that.'

'Sounds great,' he said. 'I also have work to do. How about we spend our mornings inside working and explore outside in the afternoons?'

'Excellent.'

Our days fell into a comfortable rhythm that felt a perfect fit with my disposition and needs. Sandip began his day with yoga and asked if I would like to join him. I became his willing student and looked forward to this chance to center myself before launching into the day. Following yoga, we would enjoy a light breakfast. I used these opportunities to probe a little about Sandip's life, while sharing some of mine, albeit in a somewhat edited vein.

When I first arrived in the house I noticed it lacked a table, so I wondered how I might go about my writing. But Sandip had anticipated my concern and offered a solution—a small desk with a sloping lid but no legs. I wasn't at all clear what I wanted out of this exercise but after doodling for a while, a couple of ideas began to crystallize. One had to do with the recent revelation of the presence of gay men and women in our organization and the many questions that raised. But another more private story begged to be told—my discovery of my own sexuality and all that had led me to it. The two were interrelated but the second demanded my immediate attention. From the backblocks of my mind, a tune kept forcing itself into the forefront. It was a song I had learned while teaching in a Chicago preschool years before—'When I'm on my journey there is no one else but me.' I was off and running, and for the next several days words kept flowing onto the empty pages.

After sitting for four hours at a floor desk, I was more than ready for our afternoon walks in the teak forest and down by the river that meandered through Sandip's property. The first day we ventured into the forest I was dumbstruck by the gigantic size of the teak leaves. Some were more than twice as large as my hand. I couldn't resist picking one and taking it back as a memento of this amazing visit. Years later, when I opened my notebook and found the dried leaf pressed between its pages, I was transported back to this magical place that I had been privileged to enjoy at such a pivotal moment in my life. For the first time I was able to say, 'Being gay is part of who I am and always has been. It has its ups and downs, like everything else. Now I can get on with my life as a whole person, not the confused, compartmentalized one I had once been.'

I had only one regret about this otherwise remarkable experience. Periodically, Sandip would ask how my writing was going and whether I might share some of it with him. I felt torn between two conflicting desires—to honor my host and to protect my privacy. As an Indian, even the educated, sensitive one he was, Sandip would not perceive his request as invasive or threatening to me. I had learned that it is important for Indians to know certain things about you so they can place you in their frame of reference. To outsiders, this personal probing sometimes comes as an affront, although I didn't take Sandip's questions this way. But his request presented me with another problem of much greater concern. Could I risk coming out to him? How might he react to this news? Would it spoil our wonderful time together? I had no way of knowing, so I tried to deflect his queries by saying my writing was very personal and I would prefer not to share it. I could tell this didn't satisfy his curiosity and I agonized whether and how I might accede to his request. I thought I might leave it till our last day and then spill the beans, but when the time came the exigencies of departing took over. I later had second thoughts about my reticence and began to worry how Sandip had interpreted it. Had he guessed I was gay? Was it a subject he genuinely wanted to talk to me about? Was he perplexed by my secrecy? I still think of returning one day to Kolhapur to tell him the truth and remind him what an irreplaceable gift he gave me during the precious time we shared.

* * *

On my return to Bombay, I wrote to other members of the Lavender League, describing what I had written on the role of gay and lesbian people in the Institute and suggested that they try doing the same, with a view to presenting a common paper at the Institute's global gathering the following July. I was amazed to discover that Barry, Jack and Elena had already started working on a draft paper of their own.

Not only had they begun writing, but they had also begun having discussions with people whom they thought would be sympathetic to our position. If we were to succeed in our ultimate goal, which was the assignment of gay couples, or even a basic acceptance of the presence of gay people in the organization, we had a lot of groundwork to do. The actions of my Chicago friends planted a seed in me that began to grow steadily and gave me the courage to open up to others in India. Apart from Sandy, I had not spoken to anyone about my being gay. I began to earmark certain colleagues whose friendship and respect I enjoyed, and over a meal or during a train journey I shared what I had been discovering about myself in the last couple of years. Without exception, responses were positive. Usually their one question to me was, 'Why didn't you tell me sooner?' My main question to them was, 'Would you be willing to read more about homosexuality in order to better understand it?' The answer was an unequivocal yes. I began passing on to them articles my Chicago friends were mailing me with increased regularity. Wheels were turning faster than I had anticipated.

But I was not ready to reveal my sexual orientation to everyone, particularly my Indian coworkers, since I feared they would have a more difficult time accepting homosexuality, given the entrenched prejudices against it in Indian society. However, it was not the idea or even practice of homosexuality that was so objectionable to the average Indian. It was well known that many men in India had sex with other men, although few identified as gay. As long as they kept their flings outside the confines of family life and continued to be good husbands and fathers, few questions were asked. But the moment their behavior became public knowledge, shame would kick in and all hell could break loose. Truly gay men in India found themselves in an impossible position: stay closeted and lead a double life, or come out and risk losing everything–love, support, respect, inheritance, and even life.

I would have also been foolish and naïve to assume that all my non-Indian coworkers would welcome my news with open arms. I discovered this when one of my Chicago colleagues informed me that a foreign member of our Bombay staff was antagonistic towards my homosexuality. It pained me that this particular person had this attitude, since we had known each other from our early days in the organization in Australia and I respected him a great deal.

In late 1982, while on assignment in Calcutta, my colleague's concern about my increasing absences from our residence drove him to broach the subject with Sandy.

'I'm quite worried about John,' he revealed. 'He's out so much of the time. I wonder if we may have lost him. Do you think he is visiting the ladies?'

Even though Sandy didn't know as much about me then as she did later, of one thing she was fairly certain. 'No, definitely not the ladies,' she replied.

The following year, when the emergence of a gay and lesbian group in the organization was becoming common knowledge, I heard that this colleague made it plain he was not in favor of the idea.

While I was saddened by my colleague's opposition to my sexual explorations, it didn't bother me in the same way that Henry's more overt antagonism to me did. Since our conversation in the garden, I had suspected Henry's motives with every decision he made that affected me. When he arranged for me to go to Australia on a fundraising trip for the exposition, I questioned his real agenda. On the day of my departure he made a quip about curing me of my wayward habits. Little did he realize that this actually spurred me on.

The trip proved to be of little value in terms of its purpose, but it opened my eyes wide to a gay subculture I had never known existed, let alone explored, while growing up in Australia. For the first time in my life, I discovered gay bookstores, gay baths and gay bars, none of which existed in India. Still, India retained its firm grip on me and I couldn't wait to get back. The lure of its anonymous, subterranean gay community was much more enticing than the more public façade of Australia's counterpart.

Upon my return, I made a halfhearted attempt to be reassigned to our Calcutta office to escape Henry's clutches, but I knew that my work demanded that I stay in Bombay, so I gave up on the idea. It never occurred to me that Henry might be transferred to another location instead.

Each year in July, after the annual global staff meeting in Chicago, new assignments were posted. While most people stayed at least four years in one place, all positions were up for grabs and you were expected to accept your assignment without question. Staff around the world would be on tenterhooks, eagerly awaiting the news. This year, as word trickled through to Bombay, I was not the only one taken by surprise when it was revealed that Henry would be leaving India. I had assumed he would remain at least until the exposition was over. The official line was that the exposition had added significantly to our fundraising bottom line, and required increased momentum. A new team, headed by a young American couple who had been heavily involved in the program's development abroad, was being put in place to try to meet the challenge of raising more money and undertaking extensive promotional work for the exposition. With the changeover of leadership, I now carried a lot of our common memory in India, and so was critical to the team's continuity and effectiveness.

After the announcement of Henry's pending departure, I saw less and less of him. He would disappear for several days at a stretch. I noticed that Salima was absent more as well. Salima was one of the few Muslim members of our organization and a valued member of our fundraising team. She came from a small village and was smart, attractive and ambitious. She and I had often worked together in my first couple of years and I always enjoyed her mischievous laugh. But in recent months I had had few assignments with her, while those she did with Henry had increased significantly.

Then, one afternoon, Salima arrived unexpectedly at the front door. She had come to say goodbye and collect a few things. I was stunned. Apparently, she was moving on too, although where to was unclear. After chatting for a few minutes, she said she needed to be going. I walked over to the window, glanced down, and noticed Henry slumped in the back seat of a taxi. In some ways, I was relieved to be spared the awkwardness of saying goodbye to this person whom I'd come to regard as my nemesis. Part of me felt sorry that we couldn't bring closure to our fissured relationship. Another part of me despised him for accusing me of 'illicit relations' outside the organization, while carrying on his own affair with a younger, female staff member.

Between Henry's departure and the arrival of our new team leaders, I found myself with a little time on my hands and used the opportunity to reconnect with a number of my gay friends in Bombay and catch up on my correspondence with those further afield. I also pored over a number of articles and books sent from abroad. A new word began appearing in much of the material I read. It was the acronym AIDS. I didn't have a clue what it was at first but it appeared to be a disease of the immune system that happened to show up most often among gay men. An international flight attendant was reputedly the first Indian to contract it. Within a few years, this four-letter word would become the bane of my life. But just then, innocent of the threat it represented, I carried on with my rapacious ways, stepping up the pace and increasing the danger level all the time. What had begun as an adventure was now an addiction.

HEAVEN IS IN GUJARAT

As the exposition drew closer, preparations stepped up to a feverish pace. While our staff in Delhi worked with hotel managers and travel agents to iron out endless minutiae and logistical nightmares, my own team was stretched to its limits shoring up funding and finalizing the conference brochure. I found myself traveling to cities I'd never visited, and sometimes alone, since we were all being called upon to cover more bases than usual. This created opportunities for me to indulge my own passions in ways I could only have dreamed of earlier. Gujarat, Maharashtra's neighbor to the north, was a case in point.

I had just arrived in Ahmedabad by train and checked into a shabby, third-class hotel where rooms were cheap and no questions were asked. I didn't know a soul in this rambling old city, but as I'd learned before, all I needed was one name in a new place to get me started. In this case, I had several given me by a friend in Bombay. I tried phoning the two for whom I had numbers, but as usual I didn't get through. This didn't deter me since I'd come to expect phones not to work in India. Instead,

I headed for what looked like the center of town and after a few inquiries, located the park my friend had mentioned as the most likely spot to make contact with this little coterie.

It was not the sort of place I had imagined I might connect with the gay underground. Unlike Bombay's Bandstand or Delhi's Connaught Circus, it did not lend itself easily to making covert connections. Its symmetrical gravel paths, beds of pink and orange roses, and flaming gulmohur trees gave it an openness that deterred such activities. When I entered the park through a pergola of bougainvillea, the smoke-filled haze of evening was settling over the city, bringing with it a welcome calm to replace the chaos of the day. Escaping the scrutiny of family, young couples sauntered along, eyes straight ahead and hands apart. Old men and women, venturing out of their homes in search of cooler air, shuffled by in leather chappals. And then there were the young men.

Many Indian men impressed me with their sense of style. Regardless of their income, clothes were a high priority. Usually tailor-made, they fitted better than off-the-rack varieties, whether neatly pressed white kurtas or the latest Western-style pants and shirt copied from imported fashion magazines. Gujaratis were no exception. Not all were seeking other men but you could easily recognize those who were if you were privy to their shared code of looks and gestures, often as simple as rubbing your forefinger against your nose or pulling on your earlobe. But mostly it was the flickering glance and the returned stare that communicated volumes to those tuned in to the right frequency.

A number of guys walked up and down the pathways but at this early stage, I was careful not to show too much interest in any one in particular. Given a little time, I would pare down the list to possibles, then winnow it further to preferables. Just as I was settling into my elimination process and enjoying the accompanying fantasies, I was jarred back to reality. A young man came from nowhere and sidled up beside me.

'You are new here, isn't it?'

'Yes, I've just come from Bombay.'

'How did you find this park?'

What kind of question was that, I wondered? Could he be plain-clothes CID? Something about his manner suggested otherwise. Besides, he was much too young, unless they were recruiting college students to do some of their grunt work for them.

'I asked at my hotel where I might find a park and they suggested this,' I lied.

'You staying at the Taj?'

'Oh no, I couldn't afford that. Only a cheap place near the railway station.'

My interrogator fidgeted and crossed his legs. I thought this would make him reconsider, but he seemed undeterred.

'Your good name, please?'

'I'm John. And you?'

'Santosh.'

'And what do you do in life, Santosh?'

'I'm a medical student, third year.'

His answer explained his fluent English and his direct, urbane manner. Although he wasn't the epitome of my sexual fantasy, there was something about him I admired, not least his perky style and childlike openness. I decided to let down my guard a couple of notches.

'That's interesting,' I mused. 'I have a friend in Bombay who is a third-year med student. His family's from Ahmedabad. He also mentioned this park. In fact, he gave me the names of some friends of his he said I might meet here.'

At this remark, his eyes lit up and he shifted to face me directly. 'Do you have them? May I see them?'

I hesitated a moment. The CID theory raised its scary head again. But having come to know and respect the serendipitous nature of India's gay underground, I handed him a crumpled piece of paper.

'Oh yes. I know *these* guys,' he said with a glint in his eye. 'They usually show up here around this time. One is a doctor. He has a car. If you're lucky, he might take you for a ride and show you some of the sights.'

'That sounds like fun,' I replied.

'It's bound to be,' said Santosh with the slightest grin.

Sure enough, within 20 minutes two more young men showed up, one lightly built with a thin mustache and the other a little heavier. They were walking hand in hand and their parry-riposte banter suggested they were close friends. Santosh arose and intercepted them.

'I hear we are having a mutual acquaintance,' said the slim one, introducing himself as Suresh. 'This is Moti,' he said, pointing to his friend.

We exchanged gentle handshakes.

'So how is our dear Kanti in Bombay? Behaving himself? I bet not. He wrote to say he had a new foreign friend who might be visiting these parts soon.'

I felt like a letter expected in the mail, but was pleased to find myself on a first-name basis with strangers only hours after arriving in this city. I was reminded again of the primacy of relationships in this society. Everything is predicated on them. Without them, life is a constant battle for survival. With them, doors open and privileges are granted that would not happen so easily in other parts of the world.

But this was not the time for pondering. Suresh asked if I would like to join him and Moti and a couple of other friends for a ride in his new Fiat Premier. This Italian-designed, four-door sedan was one of only two types of car manufactured in India at the time. It took obscene amounts of money to buy a car in India, not to mention infinite patience and greasing of many palms. Being a doctor from a middle-income family, Suresh had managed to acquire the vehicle early in life. He took great pride in this prize possession. Clearly, so did his friends.

All five of us piled into the compact car, sharing the limited space like sardines in a tin as only Indians can. Suresh ushered me into the middle of the back seat between two newcomers, Haroon and Nitin. They looked like college students game for anything. Out of the corner of my eye, I thought I saw them flash knowing glances at each other as I bent down to enter the car.

The first thing I noticed was that the windows were made of dark green tinted glass. You could see out but it was virtually impossible to see in. I assumed this helped with the intense glare of the sun in this dry and dusty part of the country. But it didn't take me long to realize it served another purpose.

'How are you guys doing back there?' inquired Suresh, as we drove out of the heart of the city.

Taking this as his cue, Nitin put his hand on my right

thigh as Haroon did the same on my left. Simultaneously, Nitin unzipped his fly and indicated with his eyes for me to reach inside. He must have noticed me hesitate briefly.

'It's okay. I'm clean. Have it.'

The Indian use of the imperative mood was nowhere as offensive to me now as it was when I first ran into it. But his matter-of-factness made Nitin's statement sound weirdly routine, almost perfunctory. I was lost for words. Once again, I was caught trying to reconcile a public veneer of prudery and restraint with an 'anything goes' mode of private behavior.

I was about to take up Nitin's suggestion when Haroon reached over and unzipped my fly. Without waiting for permission, he groped inside my pants and held me tightly. It was like a chain reaction rapidly getting out of control. Control was something that once defined my life but now was disappearing faster than I could say the word.

I felt my body tense as I realized how vulnerable I was, riding around in a strange city in a foreign country in the back of a car with four other guys I knew nothing about. There didn't seem to be a whole lot I could do about it; I could either grin and bear it, or let go of my fears and submit to the pleasure of the moment. I had just decided on the latter when Moti interrupted.

'You guys are awfully quiet back there.'

I glanced at the rearview mirror and caught Suresh winking at me mischievously.

Nitin let fly with a burst of Gujarati, which I interpreted to be something close to 'mind your own fucking business.' Things were fast heading in that direction.

Moti chuckled, and, as if to have the last word, Suresh

swerved the car suddenly as we went around the same traffic circle for what felt like the 47th time. Just at that moment, Nitin came like a burst of gunfire. Haroon shortly followed suit and I finished a close third. As the three of us lapsed in to a state of blissful torpidity, Suresh kept driving. We must have covered most of Ahmedabad several times over, but I was none the wiser.

When they dropped me back at my hotel two hours later, I was exhausted and elated. I trundled up the steps to my room, barely noticing my surroundings. The events of the last few hours blotted out everything else. I could hardly grasp that I had arrived in this city that afternoon, a total stranger. As I thought about it the next day, I wasn't sure the events of the previous evening had happened. Was it another of my sexual fantasies playing tricks on me? One glance at my trousers and my question was answered. How ingenious, I thought, to rig up your car so you and your friends could enjoy a little privacy. Never again could I look at a Fiat and think of it as just another car.

The next two days I was buoyant beyond belief. I sailed through them like a yacht, spinnaker unfurled, fueled by a strong tail wind and gently rolling seas. Santosh invited me to join him at a concert of Gujarati folk music the following evening. When I met him at the theater, he was accompanied by two friends, both of whom were eager to make my acquaintance. The feeling was mutual. Santosh made sure each sat on either side of me, as if to give me my pick. It was a subtle but intentional gesture. I attempted to focus on the singers and dancers on stage, but the more I tried the less I was able to. We were all engaged in a game of telepathy, shooting messages back and forth. The heaviest volume of traffic was between me and the young man to my left, Ramesh, a second-year commerce student. By the third song, the vibes were drowning out the high-pitched sounds pouring forth from the stage.

Ramesh was the stockier and more outgoing of his peers. His eyes lit up when he spoke. Each time I cast a furtive glance in his direction, he would respond with a stronger one. His right leg kept nudging my left, which left me in no illusion about his interests. This put me in a quandary, since I was Santosh's guest and I felt obliged to do as he suggested. During intermission, I excused myself to go to the toilet and when I returned, I found Santosh and Ramesh busy in conversation. As I joined them, Santosh turned to me.

'Ramesh has offered to walk you back to your hotel after the concert.'

'That's most kind of him,' I said with a swift but telling smile.

It struck me what a tremendous knack Indians have of 'doing the needful'—a stock phrase in Indian English that captured a deep-seated capacity for sweeping uncomfortable situations under the carpet, saving face, removing obstacles, and honoring the other. It described so many experiences I had in India—the company executive who offered me the use of his office phone to call my mother because he knew I couldn't afford an international call; the young man who gave up his precious ticket so I could watch the final day of an international cricket match; the accountant who invited me to dine in one of Bombay's most exclusive private clubs and use its swimming pool and other facilities. I hadn't asked for any of these; I didn't need to.

The second half of the concert seemed to drag. I feigned interest in the performance while my mind eagerly anticipated what might follow. When it ended, we all gathered outside on the steps of the theater.

'How were you liking the music?' asked Santosh.

'It was wonderful,' I replied. 'It's the first time I've heard Gujarati folk songs. They are so spirited. Thanks a lot for inviting me, Santosh.'

'No mention,' he said. There was the faintest hint of disappointment in his voice, but he was quick to cover it up. 'Ramesh will show you the way back to your hotel. It's not far from here but since you are new to Ahmedabad, you might get lost.'

I followed Ramesh like an obedient servant. When we arrived at the hotel, he went straight to the clerk at the front desk. All the way, I had been pondering how we might get Ramesh past the front desk without the clerk noticing. After all, guests were not allowed in rooms at this time, and I had not paid for a double room.

A flurry of words passed between Ramesh and the clerk. When they finished, I took my key and we proceeded up two flights of stairs to my room.

'What was that all about, Ramesh?'

'Oh, I checked if there was a way to get some whisky or beer,' he said offhandedly. 'Thought you might like a little lubrication before getting down to business.'

'Whisky or beer? Isn't Gujarat a dry state?'

'Officially, yes, but these guys have ways around that for a few extra rupees.'

'What did he say?'

'He told me to give him 15 minutes and he'd see what he could do.'

When we arrived at my room, I tried inserting the key in the lock but it wouldn't fit. I pushed it up and down and sideways but to no effect. As I fumbled with it, Ramesh slid his hand over mine and took hold of the key.

'Here, let me try,' he said.

He gave the key a hard jerk and it slipped into the lock. As it did, his other hand brushed my trousers, as if by accident. But I was beginning to realize that few things happened by accident where Ramesh was concerned. I threw him a quick glance. He raised his eyebrows as if to say, 'OK, what are you waiting for?' The room wasn't much, but what could you expect for 50 rupees a night? The metal bed frame sagged in the middle and the mattress was squishy but at least the sheets were clean. None of this bothered Ramesh, who made straight for the bed and flopped down on his back. Throwing his arms apart, he commanded, 'Come!'

Rarely had I met such initiative in my Indian sexual partners. They usually expected me to show the way but Ramesh was a different kettle of fish. I threw myself on top of him and we rolled over and over. When I pretended to pin him down, he entwined his legs with mine and turned me over. We were like wild animals in heat, going at each other with unabashed ferocity. For a moment I imagined we were a pair of lion cubs, testing each other's limits. Out of the depths of my subconscious, a strange voice rose up and called out, 'Sher-e-Gujarat!' Ramesh gave a leonine growl and I collapsed into paroxysms of laughter.

In the midst of our little drama, I nearly missed the knock

at the door. It was a polite rap at first, then it grew insistent. Ramesh leaped to his feet and stuffed his shirt back into his trousers before cautiously opening the door. After exchanging a few words with the desk clerk, he closed the door, locked it, and produced a large bottle of beer and two glasses. He poured each of us a drink and handed me mine.

'To wild lions!' he mocked, raising his glass against mine.

A half hour later, we had finished the bottle and swapped stories about ourselves. The beer had loosened our tongues but not diminished our passion. As I removed his white shirt, my eyes were drawn to the soft, unmarked skin between his neck and shoulder. It was the most delicate, seductive piece of skin I'd ever seen. I drew myself closer to him and gently placed my lips on it. Ramesh remained perfectly still as I plunged into this oasis of delight.

The night passed quickly, as we alternated between bouts of passionate lovemaking and fitful sleep. The following day, seated next to Ramesh on the floor of his family's modest home, I found it hard to reconcile that we were the same two people who had made love the night before. Now he was the dutiful elder son who had brought home a special guest. He had invited me to meet his family, and although his father was at work, his younger brother was present. From time to time, the boy shot me knowing glances, but I pretended not to notice. In my honor, Ramesh's mother had prepared a Gujarati thali, one of my favorite Indian meals. This topped off an incredible couple of days.

Regrettably, I had to leave Ahmedabad later that afternoon for Baroda, 100 kilometers south. The experiences of the last few days had lifted me up and launched me like one of the thousands of kites flying high above the city. Back in the privacy of my hotel room, tears rolled down my cheeks. What had I done to deserve such friends, who welcomed me so unreservedly into their city, their homes, and their arms? I was reminded of something written by the Australian novelist, Gregory David Roberts: 'This is not like any other place. This is India. Everyone who comes here falls in love—most of us fall in love many times over. And the Indians, they love most of all.'

Ramesh insisted on accompanying me to the railway station to make sure I had no trouble getting a seat on the train to Baroda. It was a short journey, so I was prepared to stand all the way if necessary. I'd stood over much longer distances in India in buses and trains under much more strenuous conditions. But Ramesh wouldn't hear of it. He insisted on buying me a first-class ticket to ensure that I got a seat. I was embarrassed by his generosity and protested vehemently, but he thrust the ticket into my hand. I was speechless. I stood there on the station platform, longing to fling my arms around him, but I knew this would draw attention. For a moment, we just stood and stared at each other. Then he broke the silence.

'I have one other thing for you. You might like to meet someone in Baroda. He's a really sweet guy.'

He pushed a scrap of paper into my hand. 'Vilas,' it said, along with a phone number.

'Thanks so much, Ramesh. That's very kind of you. But I couldn't imagine meeting anyone sweeter than you.'

He blushed and turned his head away. When he faced me again, I could see the moistness in his eyes. At that moment, the sound of screeching metal announced the arrival of my train. Ramesh grabbed my hand and led me down to the front of the platform where the first-class carriages would be.

'You wait here,' he ordered me.

As soon as the train came to halt, he elbowed his way into the carriage and claimed my seat. Then he shoved his head through a window.

'Come!' he yelled, and I grinned.

I jumped on the train and dumped my case under the seat. The first whistle blew so we walked to the end of the carriage where passengers were still getting on and off. Ramesh pulled me back to the closed door on the side away from the platform and gave me a quick peck on the cheek.

'Please write,' he said, as he disappeared into the crowd and headed off down the platform.

The second whistle blew and the train gave a shrug before gathering momentum. I went back to my seat in a daze and watched the city slither by. I never returned to Ahmedabad but it had carved a special place in my heart that remains there still.

* * *

When I arrived in Baroda an hour and a half later, my mind was still back in Ahmedabad, trying to comprehend and distil all that had happened. I did not feel ready to begin another adventure, and decided to focus on the several appointments I had lined up. I was also scheduled to meet a colleague from Bombay who was in town on other business. We were to share a room at the Bank of Baroda guesthouse.

When I arrived at the guesthouse, the spacious accommodations lifted my spirits. They were in stark contrast to the cheap rooms I tended to use because of limited resources. Guesthouses, whether government or private, were an exception to this. Due to our work in rural development, we were often granted free access to these establishments. The service was good, the food was fine, and the rooms always clean. The only drawback was their lack of privacy. Foreign guests were a rarity and paid a lot of attention, so you needed to be careful when inviting friends over. In this instance, there was also my young colleague to deal with.

I resigned myself to several tedious days of routine work and polite talk, but was glad to settle down after the roller-coaster ride I'd just been on. Over dinner the first evening, my roommate surprised me by announcing that he had to go to another city the next day and would stay overnight, before returning to Baroda the following day. I immediately began to fantasize how I might make best use of this unexpected opportunity.

Straight after dinner, I went to the phone in the lobby and dialed Vilas's number. No answer. I waited an hour then tried again. An older woman picked up. She had a gravelly voice but it was her Gujarati that troubled me, so I tried my limited Hindi. I gathered that Vilas was out so I promised to call back later. I replaced the phone and returned to my room where my colleague was reading a magazine. He asked me what I'd been doing, so I told him I was trying to contact a friend of a friend from Bombay.

'You seem to have connections all over this country,' he said.

'When you travel as much as I do, it's hard not to. You know how curious people are about foreigners. Sometimes I wish I weren't so damn obvious.'

After about an hour, I excused myself and went downstairs to try Vilas again. I was in luck. There was a tinge of curiosity in his voice. He no doubt guessed I was a foreigner. I told him who I was, what I was doing in Baroda, and my referral from Ramesh. At the sound of Ramesh's name, an eagerness came into his voice. 'When can we meet?' was his only question. We settled on dinner at a nearby restaurant the following evening.

Sandwiched between a dairy stall and a tailor's shop, the *Moti Sagar* was easy to miss. The downstairs was filled with wooden tables and chairs and faded pictures of Krishna bathed in an eerie blue glow. An overpowering fragrance of musk enveloped me as I walked in the front door. I glanced around and didn't see anyone corresponding to Vilas's description. I was early so decided to step outside and wait for him. As I turned to go out the door, a voice called from the reception desk.

'Excuse me, sir. Would you be Mr. John?'

'Yes I am,' I replied.

'Mr. Vilas said to look out for you. He is waiting for you upstairs.'

A steep staircase led up to the Family Room with its low ceiling, private booths, and chilling air conditioning. I looked around and saw a hand waving at me from the last booth. Its owner was one of the most beautiful looking men I'd ever seen. He beamed a welcoming smile as he extended his right hand to shake mine. His skin was warm and moist.

'Mr. John, I'm so glad you are coming.'

'The pleasure's all mine, I assure you.'

'I was worried you may have trouble finding this place.'

'Not at all,' I said. 'I'm pretty good at finding my way

around. I have developed a rule of thumb in India—ask three people, then use my best judgment.'

He laughed and his eyes sparkled. I was hooked. It wasn't just his spotless, honey-colored skin, the symmetry of his finely chiseled face, or the gentle cajoling tone of his voice. Something more intangible drew me to him.

'So you and Ramesh are friends?' I asked.

'Yes, we are knowing each other for about five years. We met at a party in Ahmedabad. He sometimes comes to visit me in Baroda.'

I was drooling to ask about more details of their visits, but propriety held me back.

'Ramesh is a very nice guy,' I said. 'We got to know each other rather well these last few days.'

I tried to keep my attention focused on Vilas but it was deflected by the arrival of the waiter. I asked Vilas to order for both of us by choosing his favorite dishes. He hesitated a moment, then looked straight at me.

'You eat veg?'

'It's about all I eat, Vilas. And I love it.'

He chose several Gujarati dishes including my favorite dessert, srikhand with sweet puris. The food did not disappoint and neither did Vilas. As far as I was concerned, he was on the menu as well and I couldn't wait to taste him.

We demolished the food with few interruptions for conversation, as Indians are prone to do. Vilas did make one comment though.

'You eat just like an Indian,' he remarked, noticing that I avoided the spoon and fork in favor of my right hand.

'When I lived in villages Vilas, I had no choice. And the

more I used my hand, the more I liked it. It makes eating a more sensual experience, don't you think?'

He didn't reply, but his approving smile communicated delight in my choice of phrase. When we had finished our meal, Vilas indicated to the waiter to bring the bill. I offered to pay but he wouldn't think of it. He led the way downstairs and out the front door.

'Would you like to come back to the guest house?' I inquired.

'You are staying alone?' Vilas asked.

I explained the situation but he still appeared a little nervous.

'You know, I work for the bank that owns this guesthouse but I have never been to this place. Only top brass go there. I might need to be careful.'

'It's okay, Vilas. I have been staying with my Indian colleague, so people are used to seeing me come and go with someone else.' It was only a 15-minute walk from the restaurant to the guesthouse. As we passed through the front gate, I waved at the chowkidar and he waved back. The front desk was closed for the night so we proceeded straight to my room. Once inside, Vilas locked the door behind us and asked if he might use the shower. When he entered the bathroom, he didn't make any effort to close the door. I stretched out on my bed, from where I had a full view of the bathroom. Out of the corner of my eye I caught a glimpse of him disrobing, first his shoes and socks, then his light blue cotton shirt and vest. His upper body was a feast for the senses with its firm contours and hairless skin. My eyes riveted on him as he slowly removed his belt, unzipped his trousers, and let them slip to the floor.

For a second he stood silhouetted against the bathroom light before stepping into the shower. I couldn't stand it any longer. I jumped up from the bed, tore off my clothes, and joined him. When I pulled back the shower curtain, he didn't seem the least surprised to see me.

Twenty minutes later, we stepped out of the shower, dripping wet. I grabbed two towels and threw one to Vilas. He began drying me so I did the same to him. Then, something from my Australian childhood triggered my memory. I took my towel, drew it back and flicked it at him, catching him on the buttocks. I raced out of the bathroom, Vilas in hot pursuit. We did several rounds of the bedroom before collapsing on the bed. It was the beginning of a long night of little sleep.

I was awakened next morning by the aarghing of crows and the honk of an auto rickshaw horn in the driveway. Vilas was not in the room. I checked the bathroom but it was empty. I was puzzled and felt abandoned. Then I glanced at the top of the dresser and found a note written in fluid handwriting with a fountain pen.

> My dear Mr. John,
>
> Thank you for such a wonderful evening. It was the very best time I have ever had with another friend. I am liking you so much. I hope it is the same with you.
>
> I am sorry I had to leave but as I told you I live with my mummy, who is alone since my father expired last year. I did not tell her I would stay away all the night and she would worry a lot about me.
>
> Mr. John, I don't want that you should go back to Bombay so soon. We must meet at least one time before you go, even

if it is not in the bed. Just to see you and talk with you again would make me so happy. Please do visit me at my work when you have a chance. I am there by 10 in the morning. We can at least take tea together and share some more.
Looking forward soooooo much to seeing you,
With warm love,
Vilas

PS. My office is Bank of Baroda, Bendi Bazaar, Lokmanya Tilak Marg, opposite Masheshwari Talkies. Ask for Vilas in foreign transfers section.

As I put down the note and brushed away the tears streaming down my cheek, I heard footsteps coming up the stairs. My colleague wasn't planning to be back until late morning at the earliest. Then I heard the key turn in the lock. My god, it was him! I grabbed the note and stuffed it in my pocket, as I raced for the bathroom and closed the door. Fortunately, Vilas and I had only occupied my bed, so there was no evidence that anyone else had been in the room. We had done our eating and drinking at the restaurant, thank goodness. The only evidence of company was two wet towels in the bathroom.

I turned on the hot water full blast and pretended not to notice my colleague's arrival. How lucky I was that Vilas had decided to leave early. I realized how perilously close I had come to a major catastrophe. I vowed to be more careful next time. But I would not have missed last night for anything. Given half a chance, I would risk everything to relive the experience.

After breakfast, I packed my case and left it at the front desk to collect later in the day. I had only one appointment and that wasn't until noon. I decided to ignore the pleas of the rickshaw-wallahs and walk into town. As I ambled along, my mind tried to catch up with me. It was brimming over with images of last night and expectations of meeting Vilas once more. But the horrible thought that it might be the last time kept weighing me down. Within hours, I would step on a train and walk out of his life, never to return. No doubt I would meet other young men who would satisfy my desires, and so would he, but the 'us' we had become in our brief time together would be a fading memory. What would he be doing 10 years from now? Married with children, I'm sure, given the good Hindu son he was. What would I be doing? Still scouring foreign lands for beautiful young men?

I found the bank with little trouble, using the tried-and-true Indian method of asking and following landmarks. I had been in many banks in India and came to loathe the experience. Banks epitomized so much of the bureaucratic tedium that riddled government and stifled business in the country. Hordes of people perfunctorily engaged in their own tasks hovered around desks and sat behind grilled windows. Boundaries of responsibility were like prison walls. To ask someone to venture outside his or her confined arena was demanding the impossible. In these pre-computer days, each entry was written meticulously in longhand in gargantuan ledgers, which a peon then took to the bank officer's supervisor for his signature, before being returned to the officer, who then gave the customer a chit to be taken to the cashier for payment. The cashier also had her own maze of procedures to navigate in order to issue money.

Here, again, being a foreigner made the process a little more bearable, especially in smaller bank branches in rural towns where the outsider was still a novelty. As soon as it was known you had entered his precincts, the branch manager would whisk you into his office, demand chai, and engage you in conversation, while his staff discreetly attended to your banking needs. Whether he has looking for diversion from his mundane routines or thought he had landed a high-paying customer, I could never quite tell. But it is another instance in India where I felt I was being honored simply for who I was.

On this bright, summery morning, however, I didn't have to jump through such hoops. I walked past the armed guard at the main door, went up to the first available teller, and asked for Vilas. She called to a peon who grudgingly shuffled off into the warren of cubicles behind the counter.

'Please, take a seat,' she said, pointing to a wooden bench. As I sat down, I tried to figure out what to say to Vilas after last night. And what of the future? How could I promise I'd see him again, when I never knew where I might be assigned next? It was an excruciating few minutes. I began to wish I had not come, but written a note instead. At that moment, a side door swung open and into the lobby strode Vilas.

'So you got my message,' he exclaimed. 'I'm so glad you came. Come, let us go and take tea.'

We went around the corner to an Irani restaurant that opened onto the street. Chai appeared from nowhere. Words, on the other hand, were awfully scarce. Vilas broke the silence.

'It was very nice, how we enjoyed last night. I've never taken bath with another guy,' he grinned.

'It was a first for me too.' Vilas shifted in his chair.

'You must be leaving today?'

'Sadly, yes. I have to be back in Bombay tomorrow.'

The glow from his face when he first met me in the bank disappeared. I was desperately trying to figure out how I might see him again, but I knew there was little chance. And even if I did, it would only mean putting off the inevitable for another six months, after which I would probably be leaving India for good. I couldn't bring myself to tell him that.

'I might come to Bombay some time. My mummy's brother is there and she visits him now and then.'

'That would be great,' I said. Then another thought flashed through my mind.

'I have to go to Delhi in a couple of weeks for a conference. I'll see if I can stop here on the way back.'

At this, Vilas perked up. He took his right hand in his left and clicked his knuckles.

'You have my phone number. Please call before you come. My mummy understands a little English.'

We sat in silence for a while, then he said, 'Well, Mr. John, I must be going back to work. I could come to the station to see you off this afternoon.'

'Thank you, Vilas, that's most kind of you, but please don't bother. And don't call me Mister. John is fine.'

He stood and offered his hand for me to shake. I did and gave it one last firm, long squeeze.

'Namaste, mera dost,' I mumbled, as my eyes moistened. Vilas walked out of the restaurant and down the street. I was so overcome with sadness, I collapsed into my seat. I have often felt sadness when parting company with close friends, but on this occasion I felt completely wiped out. The adrenaline rush that overcame me on meeting Vilas had run its course and left me like an empty shell washed up on a beach. The thought of fronting up in a public relations manager's office and soliciting one more advertisement for our brochure was the last thing I wanted to do. Instead, I started whistling a tune from a favorite Bollywood movie.

Yeh dosti, hum nahi todenge
Todenge dum magar, tera saath na chodenge
[We will never break this friendship
My strength may break, but I will not leave your side]

I suddenly became aware that people were looking at me and I snapped out my reverie. I stopped whistling and raised my hand to my mouth as if to muffle the sound. As I did so, I smelled the scent from Vilas's handshake. I inhaled and held my breath.

Two days later, sitting in a staff meeting in Bombay, I could still detect a trace of that lingering scent. Memories of Vilas and Ramesh flooded my mind, as I retreated to another world where dreams became real and pleasure overruled pain—an ephemeral world, perhaps, but one that made me delight in being alive. It had taken almost six years in India to arrive at this place, and now I didn't want to leave.

SCARED TO DEATH

My visits to Calcutta were sporadic at first, but became more frequent as time passed. The more I traveled to Calcutta, the more I came to love this shambolic place. Across India, those at the bottom of the economic pile shared a common fate, but in Calcutta their defiant, we-shall-overcome spirit reached its zenith. Self-help organizations abounded, from makeshift alleyway classrooms to the more hallowed halls of the Sisters of Charity. Our small group was one tiny drop in this mighty ocean. We focused on equipping local people with leadership, planning and learning skills to enable them to be more effective in their work.

During the day, I would help raise money to support this work. By night, my personal agenda would take over. Given our stringent working and living conditions, getting out in the evening was a perfectly natural thing to do. The regularity of my evening sorties couldn't fail to attract attention, but since my conversation with Sandy at the Marines Club, I no longer felt cloaked in guilt. I didn't need to sneak out when no one was looking; I'd calmly and unapologetically make my exit. However, Sandy's frequent admonitions to 'take care' reminded me that Calcutta by night was not without its dangers. Had she known some of the places I frequented, she might well have expressed much greater concern.

After visiting a number of Indian cities, I had grown adept at locating likely spots to make contact with young men. Apart from public toilets and crowded trains, preferred locales included parks and gardens. Calcutta was no exception. While its most expansive maidan was located close to the heart of the city, its sparse vegetation made it the least conducive to my intentions. 'The Lakes' in south Calcutta was more to my tastes. This public park, thick with trees and shrubs and sprinkled with lakes, boasted rowing clubs, a stadium, an open-air theater, and a children's park. At night, it became a favored place for men seeking trysts with men. Even smaller neighborhood parks were ripe for the picking. If, during the day, I came across a park that looked promising, I would make a mental note of it, along with the number of the tram or bus that traveled past, so I could return by night to check it out. I took great pleasure in this reconnoitering and soon learned the layout of many an Indian city—something that amazed, puzzled and impressed many of my fellow staff members.

Initial forays in Calcutta were rewarding. About a kilometer from our staff residence was a small oval that served as a sports field by day and a neighborhood node at night. On my first visit I had walked slowly several times along its perimeter to check out the crowd. I noticed a bench tucked back in a dingy corner of the park in the shadows of a bunch of eucalyptus trees. As I sat down, I saw a sturdy young man dressed in a red-checked lungi and white T-shirt making his way to the center of the field. He could have been a laborer who hauled bags of cement or flour or carried wicker baskets full of fruit and vegetables on his head. His raw physicality sent a charge through me, as I watched him chatting to another young man. An occasional chuckle punctuated their exchange but I was out of earshot. When his companion drifted off, he turned and came towards me, his lungi brushing back and forth against his leg as he walked, revealing a faint outline of his manhood. His tousled hair gave him an air of cheekiness as he strode confidently in my direction. When he was within a few meters of me, he lowered his left hand and scratched his crotch. Indian men often did this unthinkingly in public, but this was no such innocent gesture.

He passed me by, then looked back. I uncrossed my legs. That was all he needed. Turning around, he advanced towards me and lowered himself onto the bench. As he sat down, he didn't speak but his broad mouth with its upturned lips begged to be kissed. He had spun his web and I was caught.

'Ingrezi kotha bolo?' I asked to break the ice.

He shook his head to indicate he spoke no English. Instead, he just pointed to the middle of the park. At first, I didn't know what he was driving at, but I decided to follow his cue. As I stood, he grabbed my hand and led me into the center of the field. It was a friendly, playful gesture no Indian had ever offered me before. As we walked together, his body's sweaty odor washed over me. Since it was pitch dark and there was no moon, it would have been virtually impossible for someone walking along the boundary to see what was going on at the center.

When he judged we had come far enough, he sank down

onto the grass and pointed for me to follow. No sooner had I done so, than he raised one leg. I leaned over to take hold of him but he pushed my head down towards his crotch. I pulled back and shook my head. He'd have to settle for less, or nothing at all. He begrudgingly backed down and let me continue until he released his pent-up energy in a surge of unashamed delight. After reciprocating, he stood and prepared to leave. Just before he did, I kissed him lightly on the cheek. He didn't flinch, as I expected he might. Instead, he faced me and did the same, before turning around and vanishing into the night.

* * *

Return visits to Calcutta were full of such episodes, each trying to outdo the previous in ways I never imagined. My long-repressed sexual drive and the sense of anonymity I felt in Calcutta were a powerful but dangerous combination. How much longer could I go on upping the ante before being brought to heel?

During one visit, I was introduced to a group of young men who met every Wednesday after work in the back room of an electrical store. I had met one of them in a casual encounter and he invited me to come along. The owner allowed his premises to be used as a gathering place for gay friends and acquaintances in search of that most prized possession—privacy. In the dark shadows of this empty room, intimacy became possible in ways it was not anywhere else for most of these young men.

For me it had another value. It led me to develop a small but trusted group of friends who became an anchor in my turbulent life—a medical student, a teacher and a merchant seaman whose travels around the globe furnished him with tales that made the rest of us drool in incredulity. We would sometimes meet over coffee and pastries at Flury's Café or eat Chinese food in a Park Street restaurant. Our tête-à-têtes had a hint of friendly one-upmanship, as we dared to disclose with whom we did it and under what circumstances. Sometimes we shared names and phone numbers of fellow members of our little cabal. We knew we all risked something, though my Indian friends stood to lose much more than I, should things go awry. The unbearable shame such disclosure would bring and the negative reaction of family members made theirs a much less enviable situation than mine.

Most days, I tried not to think about such things. My time was precious, my calendar full. I was energized by a sense of being part of a historically important event that the exposition promised to be, and being on a vital mission of self-exploration from which I could not cut and run. Mostly, these two enterprises functioned in separate orbits but occasionally their trajectories crossed in the most surprising ways. One such occurrence stands out in my memory, if only for its serendipitous nature.

It was a warm Friday evening and I was following a lead given me by a close friend. I had spoken with the guy by phone and he welcomed my visit. Priding myself in my ability to navigate Calcutta, I told him I would go to his place. However, he lived in an outlying area of the city so it took me a lengthy tram ride and another by bus to arrive in the vicinity of his home. When I stepped down from the bus, the last of the evening light was rapidly fading from the sky, so I tried making a mental note of landmarks that would help me find my way out later.

I noticed a dim light in a tailor's shop, so I made for it and pulled out the piece of paper on which I'd written the name and address of my quarry.

'Yeh pata malum hai?' I asked as I unfolded the paper and handed it to him.

The tailor squinted in the dull light and screwed up his eyes. He motioned with his chin in the direction of the more major of two roads leading from the intersection. I asked him how far along the road I should go. He assured me it wasn't far, but when I pressed him for a number, he suggested one or two kilometers. Bracing myself for a long walk, I set off in the direction the tailor had indicated. Streetlights were few and far between, and the number of people on the street thinned the further I went down the road. After I'd gone about three blocks, I had an uneasy feeling that I was heading in the wrong direction, so I decided to check again. Ideally, I was looking for someone likely to speak English. At that moment, as if on cue, a group of three young men rounded the corner and headed in my direction.

'Excuse me,' I said. 'I'm trying to find this address. Can you help me?'

'Let me see,' said the tallest of the three, holding out his hand to receive my slip of paper. Something about his appearance rang a faint bell in the back of my mind.

'Ah yah,' he replied. 'You go about half a kilometer this way, come to a roundabout, turn left and left again. You shouldn't have any trouble finding it. Your good name, please?'

His prompt about-face took me by surprise. I obliged his first few queries then decided to play the game in reverse.

'Actually, I work in Bombay also,' he said. 'I am just visiting family here in Cal.'

When I probed further, I discovered that he was the personal assistant to the general manager of an electrical appliances firm headquartered in Bombay. The company was one I was familiar with because I had visited it with Sir James in connection with the exposition.

'How strange!' he declared. 'I know your institute. Your president visited my boss a short while back, about some rural development conference. Sir James someone-or-other, if I recall. He used to live here in Calcutta I am told. He had a young foreigner with him. We had a very nice chat about cricket and such.'

It all came back to me. We had met and talked about nine months before while waiting for his boss to admit Sir James and me. But in the dim light of this Calcutta backstreet he didn't recognize me. How unbelievable that we should meet up again, on the other side of the continent, in such circumstances. It was bizarre, almost frighteningly so. Was this a sign that something was conspiring to bring the two diverse strands of my life together into some common thread? This preposterous thought kept nagging at me. Right now, a more urgent question confronted me. Should I reveal my identity or would that only embarrass the guy? If I told him that I was the person with whom he had talked that day in the office, it would only have humiliated him. I had learned many things in my years in India and one was the Asian gift for saving face. Now, I decided, was the time to apply this lesson. I chatted for a few more minutes and thanked him for his help before heading off in the direction he had indicated.

* * *

As my nightly expeditions began to extend farther afield, I would often take a tram, then walk home to take in more of the city and maybe score an extra hit before the night ended. On one occasion, I began the long trek home with a sense of disappointment, having missed the high I now took for granted as my right each time I ventured out. As I covered block after block, my longing for a quick fix escalated. I soon noticed the quality of homes had improved from small, dilapidated houses to sizable bungalows with high walls. I had stumbled into one of Calcutta's more affluent areas. Most residences had sturdy iron gates and a gatekeeper to oversee them, sometimes with a watchdog as well. A chowkidar usually resided in a small shed just inside the gate.

As I strolled along, I noted nameplates on the walls. These were the homes of lawyers and doctors, ambassadors and government officials, as well as some who preferred to remain anonymous. One house particularly intrigued me. Brilliant orange and purple bougainvillea trailed over its walls like long, iridescent fingers. As I stopped and gazed at the spectacle in the streetlight, a slender figure materialized from the shadows behind the gate. We stared at each other for several minutes, then he motioned to me with his hand. Wearing chappals, pajama pants and a long-sleeved shirt, he must have been no more than 18 years old. He'd wrapped his head in a dark woolen scarf to ward off the damp evening air.

'Namaste,' I said.

'Russia?' he asked.

Why would he think I were Russian? Then it struck me. Probably a number of Russians lived in or visited Calcutta.

India had close ties to the then Soviet Union and more so in West Bengal with its Communist state government. Guessing me to be Russian would have been a logical choice. Perhaps there was a Russian residence or consulate nearby. My mind played mental leapfrog.

'No. Australia,' I replied.

'You live near?'

'Not far.'

'What you like?' he asked in a typically cut-the-crap fashion I had come to admire in Indians of his ilk.

Stepping up to the plate, I swung the bat for all it was worth.

'I like you.'

I couldn't believe I'd said it. 'You must be out of your crazy, sex-starved mind,' I thought to myself. He wasn't much to look at. I didn't know a thing about him; he didn't know anything about me. He didn't need to. I was desperate for one last fling.

'How much?' he asked.

'Ten rupees,' I said optimistically.

'Bees,' he replied, doubling the price.

Just as we were about to settle on a deal, a dark green Fiat swung around the corner and entered the driveway opposite. The gatekeeper looked at me nervously.

'Sahib coming soon. You come tomorrow night, same time.'

'Okay,' I said, reluctantly.

All the next day, as I visited companies and sat in staff meetings, my mind was focused on our pending rendezvous that night. Having it off with a gatekeeper late at night behind the high walls of a wealthy estate would be another first. Fantasies of E M Forster's *Maurice* started playing themselves out in my imagination. The uniqueness of it tantalized me, although my rational mind told me I'd be wiser to avoid it.

As evening approached, I lingered around the house longer than usual to fill in time. At about 9.30 pm I headed out and had little trouble finding the place. It was only about a 15-minute walk from our residence and I had kept a mental note of the connecting streets. When I came to the corner, I could hardly contain my rising sense of anticipation. But I also began to feel apprehensive. Unlike my usual hit-or-miss escapades, this felt too programmed. The odd Ambassador taxi idled up and down the main road and an occasional pedestrian passed by. I slowed down and walked along the opposite side of the street and back again. There was no sign of the gatekeeper. I felt nervous but was not about to quit. I went up the block and back again, before taking up a position opposite the gate under the streetlight where I had stood the night before.

Out of nowhere, a brown jeep loaded with half a dozen men screeched to a halt at the curb about a meter away from me. The person in the front passenger seat shone a blinding flashlight in my eyes.

'Who are you?' he snapped.

Who were *they*?

'I'm a visitor to Calcutta.'

'Where are you from?'

'I'm from Australia but I live in Bombay.'

'What are you doing here?'

'I went for a walk and got lost.'

'Why were you walking up and down in the same place?'

'I was trying to figure out how to get home.'

'Where are you staying?'

'Beck Bagan, I think it's called.'

The one holding the flashlight turned to his driver and spoke a few sentences in Bengali. Foreigners didn't stay in Beck Bagan, known for its squalid bustees and nearby public market. My answer only raised more questions. I tried to say as little as I could while not lying, in case my answers should rebound on me later. It would be easy for them to verify my address. I decided to go on the offensive.

'Can you tell me how to get to Beck Bagan?'

My interrogator paused, as if caught off guard. Another rapid discussion ensued. I kept peering towards the gate, expecting to see the young gatekeeper, but he never showed. What was his role in all this? Had he set me up? Was it pure chance the jeep came along at this time? Questions outnumbered answers. Then it dawned on me; I was in the middle of my first encounter with the Calcutta police—the jeep, the flashlight, and the lathis that two men in the back of the vehicle were carrying. My stomach contracted. Bribery might be my only weapon, but I had no money. If I tried this tactic, they would no doubt accompany me to my residence, where I would have to suffer the embarrassment of explaining to my colleagues what had happened, and hope that payment of money would bring closure to this nightmare. Just as I was imagining spending the night in a police lockup, a brusque voice shook me back to the present.

'Get out of here before I change my mind,' he ordered me.

'Which way did you say to Beck Bagan?'

'Two streets up and left. Now go!'

My hands were shaking as I took off up the street at a brisk trot. It wasn't until I heard the jeep spin around and speed off down the street that my breathing returned to normal. Why had he decided to let me go? Did I actually convince him I was a stupid tourist? Was my naiveté so transparent that I wasn't worth troubling with? Whatever the reason, I'd been let off the hook, like I was that night at Bombay Central station. It was time to do another puja to Lord Ganesh. I was pleased I had managed to keep cool under pressure, but one thing kept eating away at me—I was willing to override my intuitions to play it safe for the sake of one more conquest.

* * *

I worked on the principle that trying to express oneself in the local language, regardless of ability, was better than not trying at all. Living and working in Maharashtra's villages, I had acquired a rudimentary level of Marathi but when I began moving around the country this was of little use. In offices and boardrooms, English was taken for granted, but on the road and in rural areas, it wasn't. I would try to get by with a smattering of Hindi scoured from magazines, films, taxi-drivers, beggars and interminable village planning consultations. In Calcutta, the challenge of mastering Bengali was one language too many, so I usually fell back on the high level of English spoken there. If I had just stuck to this rule, I probably would not have found myself one night fearing for my life.

My growing craving for instant sexual satisfaction had led me to expect that I could find it whenever and wherever I wanted. This week I wanted it more than most. Work had been trying. Visits to companies for financial support had yielded only hollow promises. My third meeting with a leading tea exporter had produced two kilos of premium Darjeeling second flush tea, but not a single rupee. A top-ranking Tata executive, who had promised me he would ask one of India's leading artists to auction one of his paintings in support of our work, failed to deliver once again. Frustration had set in and I was feeling unusually depressed. By Saturday night, I was ready to break loose.

Our foreign staff had grown used to my evening absences and mostly left me to my own devices. Occasionally, they would ask if I would like to join them for a few beers at a local bar, but I was not much for small talk and forfeiting a night of cruising came as a major sacrifice these days. On this particular evening I slipped on my olive pants and matching striped cotton shirt and headed out the front door. This outfit was my standard evening garb, tailor-made to fit my slim frame. When I changed into it, I felt like a whole new person. My night binges were my way of trying on a new self and these clothes were a key part of that. They didn't go unnoticed by others either.

'Hey Burbs, wearing your green battle fatigues again!' Sean said with a smirk. I couldn't help think how apt a description this was.

Instead of taking a tram to the heart of town, I decided to walk. I wanted to immerse myself in the evening's sensory extravaganza. Bells twanged as rickshaw-wallahs forced their way through oncoming traffic; horns tooted as overloaded trucks rumbled along tramlined roads; loudspeakers shrieked popular film songs. None of this bothered me anymore. I almost welcomed its grating dissonance.

Stepping outside, I looked up and down the street and set off for the maidan at a brisk pace. In the heart of this urban jungle, the spacious maidan seemed an anomaly, but a welcome one at that. On one side of this vast park, the bustling Chowringhee Road with its crumbling buildings and snarling traffic was like a retaining wall struggling to hold back the roaring floodwaters of the city's burgeoning masses. On the other hand, its utter emptiness threatened to swallow you whole. When I reached the maidan, I did a quick survey of my usual haunts and spotted one or two prospects, but none too interesting. The night was still young so I could afford to pass up those who didn't strike my fancy, and keep pursuing my quest for the perfect young man.

This night was a write-off. Where were all the young men? It wasn't Diwali or Durga Puja. Were they sick, consumed with family matters, or what? Maybe I should have gone out with my colleagues after all. Before calling it quits, I decided to take one last stroll along Chowringhee Road. When I came to the Grand Hotel, I hesitated a moment before entering its spacious lobby. Once Calcutta's finest, this imposing building was a local landmark. Boxwallahs and politicians, maharajas and film stars had all graced its stately rooms, not to mention thousands of servicemen during World War II. But five-star hotels were not my scene. Although foreigners formed a large part of their clientele, I always felt strangely conspicuous, expecting any minute that a security person might ask me what I was doing there. Based on my experiences in other Indian luxury hotels, this would not have been out of the question.

I sat down for several minutes, surveying the comings and goings of Indians and foreigners alike. Nothing registered on my gaydar.

Disappointed, I made for the door. As soon as I was outside, the clammy night air enveloped me like a damp shroud. It had a raw edge to it that ratcheted up my senses several levels. Air conditioning was something I was neither used to, nor welcomed. Now I was back in the real world of most Calcuttans, with its discordant sounds and foul smells. I pretended to be interested in window displays and tried to ignore the hawkers who had settled down on the pavement for the night under the verandah's wide overhang. It was probably about 9 pm. Just as I was about to turn into a side street, a rickshaw-wallah called out to me.

'Oh sahib, you want ride?'

'No thanks.'

'You want hashish? Very good hashish. Very cheaply.'

'No.'

'You like young girl? I know beautiful young girl, bahut…'

His theatrical gestures made it amply clear which part of the female anatomy he had in mind. I don't know why, but at that moment I decided to change languages and practice my limited Hindi. I also made another switch.

'Ladki nahi. Ladka?'

My sexual preference never raised his greying eyebrows. His eyes lit up. Persistence had paid off. 'I know good boy. Very clean. No problem.'

'Kitna paise?'

'Ek sau rupaye.'

I laughed at his attempt to extort 100 rupees from me. I

had 60 rupees on me at the time, 40 in my money pocket and 20 in my shoe, for emergencies.

'Pachas,' was his next offer.

'Tees,' I countered.

He glowered and I began to walk away.

'Sahib, idhar ao,' he called, motioning me to him.

I stood for a moment, unsure what to do. Should I trust this guy? Where was he taking me? Would he demand more money once he delivered me? Should I back down while I have a chance? But other voices were shouting to be heard over and above these. Go on, just do it. You'll never know if you don't give it a try. Be a devil. Don't hold back. You might never do such a thing again.

Trembling inside, I walked timidly towards the rickshaw and sat down. He whirled the cart around and gave it a hearty pull. As we set off, the first few streets were familiar but after 10 minutes I couldn't recognize any landmarks. We turned from one street to another, each narrower than the last. I could only tell that we were in a bazaar district because shops and food stalls were open. He turned right into a dark lane and pulled up outside a towering concrete wall, facing a giant wooden gate that looked like it would take a tank to break down. He dropped the handles of the rickshaw on the ground and pointed with his nose at the gate.

'Ladka andar hai.'

As I stepped off the rickshaw, the driver rubbed two fingers against the thumb of his right hand. I was confused. Was he asking for the 30 rupees I'd agreed to pay for the services of a young man?

'Kitna?' I asked

'Das rupaye.'

I handed him the money. He pocketed it and made for the gate, giving it a sharp rap with his fist. I heard the scraping sound of an iron bolt being rolled along. The gate protested as it was pushed open and the face of an old man filled the narrow gap. The rickshaw-wallah and chowkidar exchanged a few words. I began to have second thoughts about what I was getting myself into. The building looked more like a Moghul fort than a bordello. How would I get out of here if I needed to? The walls were too high and too smooth to scale. The gate was impenetrable. The chowkidar disappeared for a couple of minutes. Then the gate opened again and he motioned me to enter. I hesitated, turned around, and stared at the rickshaw-wallah. He looked at me blankly, as if to say, 'Well, go on. What are you waiting for? This is what you came for, isn't it?'

Inside the compound, the otherwise bright street lights dimmed to an eerie gloom. Stone steps led from the middle of a gravel pathway to rooms on either side of a narrow corridor. So this is a Calcutta brothel, I thought. Nothing like the grilled cages of the cheek-by-jowl hovels in Bombay's Kamathipura Lane. An overweight, middle-aged man dressed in a dirty white kurta came bustling towards me. As he opened his mouth to speak, I noticed the familiar red stains of betel nut smudged across his lips. His breath reeked of cheap Indian whisky.

'Upar!' he barked, gesturing me to go upstairs.

I ascended the staircase and walked down the corridor. He pointed to the second room on the right. As I entered, I noticed there was a key lock on the outside and a bolted lock on the inside. The room was about six meters by three, with a rope charpoy covered with a thin stained sheet in one corner and a rickety wooden chair in the other. There were no windows. A lone bulb suspended from the ceiling cast a yellowy light over the room. The place stank of sour milk and urine. Above a rusted spittoon, red splotches flecked the wall. I felt I was in a prison cell, not a bedroom. My stomach churned. Alarm bells started ringing in my brain. The idea of having sex evaporated. A voice from within bellowed, 'Get out of here now!'

I was about to act on my impulse when the door burst open and three men walked in. The man who had ushered me from the gate was flanked by two others, younger and in better shape. They glanced at me, then at each other. One had a sneer that caused my heart to beat faster.

'You want boy?' asked the older man.

Before I could say 'no thank you, there must be some horrible mistake,' he continued.

'Two hundred rupees.'

'Two hundred rupees! The rickshaw-wallah said 30 rupees,' I protested. 'I don't have 200 rupees. I only have 30. Look.'

He glanced at his two flunkies, who took a step closer. I fumbled in my pocket and produced three 10-rupee notes. Before I knew what was happening, they were ripped from me. At that moment, my left cheek stung as a hand walloped my face. I nearly lost my balance. I was sweating like the Ganges in flood. Words failed me, but I managed to get one out.

'Badmash!'

Where that word came from I'll never know. Maybe one of the larger-than-life cinema billboards from which the villain leers with burning eyes and clenched fists. That was enough to produce another blow to my right cheek that sent my head whirling. My fear level shot up. No one except the rickshaw-wallah knew where I was. I could end up like so many other unidentified corpses in the lower reaches of the Hooghly and no one would be any the wiser. I panicked.

The older man turned to his offsiders and shot off a few phrases in Bengali. The two younger men approached me. I instinctively prepared to protect myself, but as I did so, one grabbed my arms and the other rifled through my pockets. Not finding any cash, they turned to their boss, who spat out a mouthful of words.

'Sala jhutha kahin ka! Mujhe banata ha?'

Translation escaped me but the intent of his words did not. Another flurry of Bengali followed. One of the men went out of the room, leaving the door slightly ajar. The other threw me a menacing stare and started pacing up and down. Fear grabbed hold of me, a more terrifying, more total fear than I had ever known.

Then, to my utter surprise, the man who had exited the room returned with a boy in tow. He would have been no more than 11 or 12, barefoot and dressed in striped pajamas. I was stunned. Then it struck me. While negotiating with the rickshaw-wallah I had used the Hindi word 'ladka,' which means 'boy.' My mind raced to look for a way out. While the three men were absorbed with the new arrival, I took a deep breath and made a dash for the door. I flung it open, tore along the corridor and leaped down the steps two at a time. Behind me I could hear voices yelling 'pagal' and 'sanki.' Speed was my only self-defense. I always had an inkling that my short-lived career as a high-school sprinter might come in handy one day. That day had arrived. Calling on all my reserves, I raced to the gate, my last but formidable hurdle to rid myself of this vile place.

The chowkidar stared in disbelief as I tore across the yard in his direction. He rose from his seat, then looked up to the top of the stairs. The two younger men stood there yelling at him. My adrenaline shot up. The old man looked confused by this extraordinary scene he found himself caught up in. As I neared him, I screamed, 'Open the gate!'

He began to do so, then pulled back. The two men were at the bottom of the stairs and closing in fast. I knew I couldn't handle both of them. In desperation, I pushed aside the old man, who went tottering to the ground. I slammed back the metal bolt, thrust open the gate, and hurled myself through the gap. One of my pursuers went to the aid of the old man while the other lunged towards the open gate. Just then, I slammed it so hard it nearly came off its hinges. A piercing scream soared above the hubbub of the street as the gate smashed into his fingers. I lurched forward and rolled onto the ground. Several passersby ran to my assistance. I stood up, shaking, speechless. My head spun; I felt as though my bowels were about to let loose. Without looking back, I headed down the lane to the corner, turned into the main street, and fled into the night.

BETRAYED

Unlike my earlier visits to Calcutta, this time I left with a heavy heart and a quickening sense of vulnerability. Until now, I had reveled in taking risks with an adolescent naiveté that had fooled me into believing I was somehow protected from the vagaries of life. The abortive visit to a brothel and my run-in with the plain-clothes police had smashed that illusion. My willingness to keep pushing the limits for the sake of another fleeting thrill had exposed me to dangers I had ignored in my callow pursuit of excitement. If my time in India was a rite of passage to adulthood—albeit rather belated—I had just taken a major step towards maturity.

That step, however, came at a price. It shattered my self-image and called into question my story about myself. My sexual dalliances notwithstanding, I believed I was fundamentally a decent human being, driven more by others' demands than my own desires. I was a team player and always ready to go the extra mile. Regardless of the task, I put my heart and soul into it. If anything, I was a bit too obsessive about most things. I was also a slow starter but, as if to compensate for that, a strong finisher. Once I overcame my initial apprehension and tentativeness to take on a task, I was in it for the long haul and pursued it with relentless zeal. It had never occurred to me that this might also be true of my newfound quest for sexual gratification, and perhaps to my detriment. The 'making up for lost time' story had been a shot in the arm to get me out the door, but now I was up and running it was wearing a little thin. Maybe it was time to take stock, pull back, and reassess where I was going. At least, that's what my rational, left brain advocated. But it proved little match for my more powerful right brain that kept on harking, 'You're on a roll, don't stop now!'

And I didn't. A couple of weeks after returning to Bombay, the memory of the events in Calcutta began to recede. Most nights I hit the beats, where the lure of new places and new faces was as strong as ever. So, too, was my imagination, which was working overtime to come up with more creative ways to meet young Indian men. No longer was I satisfied to limit myself to casual one-on-one encounters. I started looking for more prolonged engagements in less frenetic settings. Fantasies of romping around in peaceful, rustic domains played havoc with me. Such visions had to be tempered by hard reality, which for me meant limited funds, little time away from work, and communal living. Such realities dominated, but I became more adept at finding ways around them.

This happened one day during my visit to a charitable trust that had been a regular supporter of our work. The director made it clear that while they couldn't provide more than their standard donation, they might be able to help in other ways. In the popular resort town of Lonavala, midway between

Bombay and Pune, their trust ran a holiday home for those who couldn't otherwise afford such a luxury. Since we lived and worked on minimal stipends, our staff qualified to stay there. We only needed to contact the director and he would make the arrangements. It felt too good to be true. I thanked him for his kind offer and began to think how we might make use of it. On the way home in the bus that afternoon, a wild idea flashed through my mind—this could be an ideal opportunity for me to spend a few days with friends. Accommodation would be free and travel costs minimal. No one would know that my companions weren't actually my coworkers. I only had to make sure my colleagues didn't find out. It was a risk, but one I was willing to take for the sake of the rewards it promised. A year ago, even six months earlier, such an idea would never have occurred to me.

Questions swirled around in my head. When could I do it? Who should I ask to join me? What kind of mix of guys would work? As I went about my daily tasks, these questions remained in the forefront of my mind. Diwali was coming up and our Indian staff usually took time off to go home to visit their families. It would be an ideal opportunity for me to pursue my little scheme, if I could arrange it in time. From a public phone out of earshot of curious colleagues, I called the director and asked for a four-person room for three days. He pointed out that Diwali was one of their busiest times, but he would check with the manager of the home and get back to me. I offered to call him instead the following week.

The immediate challenge was deciding who to invite. If I started flipping through my rapidly expanding address book, I wouldn't know where to stop. I was still mulling this over a couple of days later when I ran into Akbar at the Bandstand. My first gay Muslim friend in India, he was quietly spoken and refined, and lived in a small, two-room apartment. In one of those rooms we had shared a sweltering Sunday afternoon together. I remember Akbar closing the wooden windows that allowed air and light into the room, before rolling out a thin mat on the hard wooden floor. There were prices to pay for intimacy in India, and comfort was one of them. I held a hidden admiration for Akbar, not purely for his wiles as a seductive lover, but also for his wisdom and common sense. More than once, I called on him for advice, which he sometimes gave without my asking. But he possessed one quality I valued above all others. Not only did he mix with gay Muslims, but he counted Hindus, Christians, Sikhs and others among his friends. This was to prove most valuable as I broached my plan to him.

'Sounds like fun,' was Akbar's first response. 'Who else are you thinking of inviting?'

'Well, that's a little tricky. I was wondering if you might be able to help me figure it out. Getting the right combination of guys to share a room for two or three days isn't easy. We'd all have to be comfortable with one another.'

'Let me think about it,' he said with the sagacious look of an old imam. 'Why don't we meet here next Saturday night and discuss it further.'

When I met Akbar the following week, he had done exactly as he promised, and more. Not only had he thought about other possible roommates, he had met one and run the idea by him. This was Amul, a Hindu friend of his I knew vaguely and looked forward to knowing more intimately. He exuded

Bollywood good looks with charm to spare. He had told Akbar to 'count me in,' pending a possible family conflict with the date. That left one slot to fill. Akbar's recommendation was Kelvin, a smart-looking young Christian guy who was on good terms with both Akbar and Amul. He rivaled Amul in appearance and was about the same age. Akbar offered to sound him out.

Diwali was rapidly approaching and I hadn't heard from the director of the trust. Instead of phoning, I decided to drop in on him late one afternoon after finishing the day's appointments. After a 20-minute wait, I was ushered into his office. He apologized that he hadn't done anything about my request. I started to despair. I would have egg on my face if I had to back down now. Looking him straight in the eye, I told him so and he took the hint.

'I will do one thing. I will call right now to see if there is a room available,' he said.

Picking up the phone, he asked his secretary to place a lightning call to Lonavala and then ordered chai for both of us. Not surprisingly, the chai arrived a lot sooner than the call. Despite their name, lightning calls could take hours to come through, depending on the weather, the day of the week, the time of day, and certain planets being in alignment with others. After about half an hour, the phone rang and a swift exchange in Marathi left me wondering about my fate. After a bundle of achcha's and ji haan's and tilting his head back and forth, the director put down the phone and turned towards me.

'You are lucky, Mr. John. There is just one room available during that time, but it only has three beds. Would that be OK?'

'No problem,' I replied nonchalantly.

He had me sign the usual plethora of forms and I was relieved I didn't need to divulge the names and addresses of my companions; I could sign everything on behalf of my party. The pieces were falling into place nicely.

As Diwali grew closer, my sense of anticipation heightened. Three days and nights of relaxing with a group of young gay men was more than I could have hoped for. I kept checking with Akbar to see if our other two friends were still a go. Kelvin was a definite and Amul a probable. Akbar and I decided to travel together to Lonavala by bus and the other two would come by train. Right to the last minute, I had a nagging feeling that something would go wrong. I prayed a silent prayer to Lord Ganesh to remove any obstacles that might frustrate my plans.

When I met Akbar at the Bombay bus terminal, he looked as though he had just taken his morning bath. His mustache was sharply trimmed, his kurta was blinding white, and his recently shaven face gave off the beguiling fragrance of sandalwood.

'Assalamu alaikum!' I greeted him.

'Wa alaikum assalam,' he returned, with a smile spreading across his face. Something told me that he was looking forward to this adventure as much as I was.

Being a Friday, he had come straight from the mosque. We had little trouble finding a bus, since Lonavala was on the main road to Pune and buses were frequent. Akbar took charge and bought our tickets. The journey passed quickly, the air cooling as the bus rumbled its way up the Western Ghats. We chatted off and on, but I was consumed with one worry.

'Do you think Amul and Kelvin will come?' I asked.

'I'm sure they will,' he said. Then, as if to cover his tracks, he added 'Insha Allah!'

The holiday home was a large, two-story building with a quadrangle in the middle that gave it the air of a boarding school. On every pillar and bulletin board, in Marathi and English, were lists of rules governing the institution—times for meals and room cleaning, prohibitions against loud noise and bad language, exhortations against wasting electricity and water, night curfews, and more. It felt as though we had stepped into a reformatory or convent. How on earth would my companions take to this? When I had heard 'holiday home' I hadn't imagined anything like this and I'm sure they hadn't either.

We checked in at the office and picked up our room key. I told the manager we were expecting two others and that we would not be taking meals, except breakfast. I was sure we would want to spend as much time as possible outside the place, except at night. But just then, we had several hours before the others arrived, so Akbar and I wasted no time in getting re-acquainted in the luxury of our own private room, before drifting off into a mindless slumber. When we awoke, it was half an hour before the scheduled arrival of the train, so we promptly dressed and took an auto-rickshaw to the station. I was still wondering if our companions would show. Five minutes before the train was due, I began pacing up and down the platform. I looked at Akbar and grimaced.

'I sure as hell hope God does will it!'

As the train slowed to a halt, bodies poured out of its crowded doorways like water from a spigot. Akbar and I glanced along the platform as we tried to spot our two friends. Seconds stretched into minutes as we scanned the crowd. Then, in a burst of glee, Akbar exclaimed 'Over there!' I turned and saw Amul and Kelvin walking hand in hand down the platform towards us. My heart soared.

For the next two and half days, the four of us indulged in one another's company with unrestrained delight. The pressures of our tedious daily lives evaporated as we luxuriated in delectable meals, went for long walks in the nearby hills, and shared beds at night. It was not uncommon in India for a group of young men to spend time together, but if the manager had even had a hunch about the nature of our relationship, he would have kicked us out without the slightest hesitation. Worse, word of this would undoubtedly have got back to the director and the trust's ties with the Institute may have been permanently severed. In spite of this weighing on me, I chose to risk it and allow my fantasy to play itself out.

On our final night, we decided a movie was in order. There were two shows playing in town and choosing one proved less difficult than I imagined. In celebration of our religious diversity, we chose the Bollywood classic, *Amar Akbar Anthony*. This story of three young brothers abandoned by their father and raised in different families—one as a Hindu, another as a Muslim, and the third as Christian—took India by storm. It projected the Indian actor, Amitabh Bachchan, into superstardom. By a miraculous turn of events that only a Bollywood movie can produce, the three brothers are reunited as young men when they donate blood in aid of their ailing mother. The plot overflows with the usual astonishing twists and turns, as forces for good and evil vie for supremacy and flamboyant song-and-dance routines take the audience back and forth from the so-called real world to the utterly surreal. It was like a metaphor of our time together.

* * *

After our romp in Lonavala, I began to see a lot more of Kelvin. This tallish young man with puckered lips, olive skin and a gently muscular body conveyed a hint of his mixed Indian-Portuguese ancestry. He was my Adonis. The very thought of his name aroused pleasure in me. He was quite aware of his fine physique, but unlike so many young Indian men he didn't seem to flaunt it. But there was more to Kelvin than his abundant good looks. Being a Christian in this society meant being part of a minority that was often sidelined. Being gay made him a minority within a minority.

Over the next few months, we met as frequently as we could. We would squeeze in lunch when I was doing calls alone or meet at the Bandstand when our schedules permitted. Once, when I had a few days off, I managed to get us a room in the nearby Catholic hostel at short notice. As soon as we had checked in, we went straight to our room. Although I was salivating in anticipation of what was to come, I sensed Kelvin wasn't, but I couldn't quite put my finger on it. As I took hold of his hand and lowered him to join me on the bed, my instincts proved correct.

'Do you mind if we don't have real sex today?' he asked.

'Real sex. What do you mean?'

'You know, like we usually do, with a condom and all.'

'Sure, if you'd prefer,' I said, trying to figure out what was on his mind.

As I looked directly into his dark, soft eyes, he turned his face away.

We lay down on the bed and I began undressing him. Kelvin obliged but somewhat reservedly. We were down to our underwear when he broke the silence between us.

'You ever had any sexual diseases?' he asked.

I stopped in the middle of peeling off his white vest.

'Yes, I've had some. Have you?'

'No, not yet, luckily.'

He paused, looked away, then turned back towards me.

'If you have them, do you still have sex with guys?'

'No, I always wait until the sores have healed. That way, it protects my partner and doesn't aggravate my own problem.'

'So you don't have anything now?'

'No. Why do you ask?'

My question was met with a brief silence. Kelvin rolled over on his side, as I waited for his reply.

'I...I met someone who said he knows you. He told me that you have sex with a lot of guys and that I should be careful.'

I searched my mind for this mysterious informant, but the futility of the exercise became apparent. There were so many guys I'd had some form of sexual experience with in the last couple of years that it could have been any of dozens in Bombay alone. I decided to ask Kelvin directly, even though I knew it was embarrassing for him.

'Who told you that?'

He hesitated again.

'Oh, some fellow I met at the Bandstand. I don't remember his name.'

It was obvious Kelvin was stalling, either to protect himself or to avoid incriminating his source. I decided not to push further and he seemed relieved. We resumed our lovemaking, but he lacked enthusiasm. This wasn't at all how I'd envisaged things would go. For the next few days, my mind was preoccupied with searching for the identity of the person who had soiled my relationship with Kelvin, with no success.

Then, one morning as I was riding the bus down to the Fort area, it came to me. There was only one person who had information about my sexual diseases—the doctor who had been treating me for a couple of years now. I was sure I was right. The last time Kelvin and I had met, he had asked me where he, as a gay man, could go in Bombay for a health check-up without any risk of recrimination. Knowing few physicians, I had volunteered the name of my doctor. Now I was annoyed with myself and even angrier with the doctor for revealing such information about one client to another. Before the bus reached Flora Fountain, I decided to go straight to the doctor's office and confront him. His clinic was on the first floor of a run-down building in a part of the city better known for bicycle repair shops and stationery stores than medical services.

The first time I contracted a sexually transmitted disease in India, I didn't know where to go for help. I certainly didn't wish to consult my local doctor around the corner from our residence, for fear of revealing too much about my personal life. The only other doctor I knew was a friend of the Institute who volunteered his services in villages where we worked outside Bombay. He was one of those saints who would go to any length to assist those less fortunate than himself. He also ran a clinic in the heart of the red-light district a few kilometers from our residence. Given this location, he probably knew more about treating sexually transmitted diseases than most doctors, but I couldn't imagine going to him for help—not that I ever thought he would berate me or deliver moralizing sermons. I just didn't want to place him in the invidious position of having to harbor such a secret.

The answer to my dilemma came in the form of a large sign in English and Urdu that caught my eye as I rode the double-decker buses to the Fort area. In the heart of a Muslim neighborhood, it stood out from the hundreds of other signs because of its mammoth size and the two large red crosses at either end of it. At the center were the words: 'Expert in Vanereal Diseases and Sexual Disfunction'. When my complaint became bad enough, I decided this was the place to go. So paranoid was I that someone would see me entering this establishment, I alighted from the bus several blocks before and made a sudden dart into the building. The middle-aged doctor took one glance at me, gave me an injection—the universal cure-all in India—and sent me on my way. The cost was minimal, the experience humiliating.

By contrast, my current doctor seemed like a godsend. He was a little closer to my age, was widely traveled, and himself gay. I had been referred to him by another friend who told me that he treated a number of gay men in Bombay. When I first met him, I was pleased I could discuss many subjects with him, not only my health—something many Indian doctors didn't deign to do with their patients—but other matters close to my heart as well. I even imagined at times that we might go out to dinner or have a friendly drink. He belonged to a more discreet and loftier stratum of Bombay's gay scene than I did.

He went to private parties among the professional set and flew abroad on holidays, reporting back to me on the state of gay life in exotic parts of the world. I kept asking him to introduce me to some of his friends, in the hope I might graduate from the street scene. He vowed he would, but never did.

I burst into his office and poked my head through the small opening that served both as a reception desk and a dispensary for medications. The young man who worked there had come to know my face. He was polite but somewhat disdainful in his manner. He no doubt knew of his boss's sexual tendencies and projected them onto most of his male clients as well.

'I'd like to see the doctor please,' I said.

'Doctor sahib is not in. He's taking lunch.'

It wasn't usually necessary to make appointments in advance when consulting a local doctor in India; you simply showed up and waited your turn. I glanced at my watch. It was 1 pm. Lunch could take any amount of time, especially if a siesta followed it. I toyed with the idea of returning later, but given my state of mind I decided to wait. Two other people had been waiting before me. I had long since become resigned to waiting in India and always brought some reading material to help fill the void. Forty-five minutes later, the doctor ambled in. He cast a quick glance in my direction and entered his consulting room. The first patient only took a few minutes, but the second was with him for close to 20. Finally, it was my turn.

'So what's the problem today?'

I was in no mood for small talk and so went straight for the jugular.

'I referred one of my friends to see you a couple of weeks

ago. Kelvin was his name. Do you remember him?'

He hesitated for the briefest moment before answering.

'Yes, I think I do.'

'Kelvin told me that someone had warned him not to have sex with me because I am always getting diseases.'

'Sounds like he may have been given some good advice.'

'I was puzzled how he knew so much about me.'

'I'm sure your reputation is around this town by now. You don't exactly melt into the crowd, do you? And you know how cliquish the club is.'

'Maybe, but it struck me as rather coincidental that Kelvin received this advice after coming to you for help.'

I was warming up to deliver my final punch. The doctor blinked several times, as if maneuvering to avoid the blow. It was too late to pull back. He'd decided to stand his ground. His face turned a brighter shade of pink.

'You are always coming in here with one thing after another because of your sexual escapades. What did you expect me to say to him? Nothing?'

'I'd have expected you to be more discreet in giving advice and naming names. What about the Hippocratic Oath, medical ethics and client confidence?'

'How dare you lecture me about how I should conduct my business! You foreigners think you can come here and act so morally superior.'

I was shocked at how much he despised me, while all the time he'd given me the impression that we had a much more genial relationship. I had totally misread him. Before I could reply, he continued.

'You're always picking up boys off the street. You don't

know where they've been or what they've got. Why don't you keep to those a little more educated and sophisticated.'

That was all I needed to send a parting shot across his bow.

'Now who's doing the lecturing? Don't you think I've wanted to meet guys like that? I don't have connections like you do in those circles. You have always been telling me about your friends and their wonderful parties and offering to introduce me to them, but you never have.'

'Can you blame me?'

'Yes, I do!'

With that, I turned on my heels and stomped out of his clinic. As I raced down two flights of stairs, I wondered how many other young men in Bombay he'd warned about me. This was not the kind of reputation I was proud of, although maybe one I deserved.

***

As devastating as this experience was, it didn't deter me from continuing my evening sorties, although every time I met someone I knew, I wondered whether he had been advised to steer clear of me, either from my doctor or via the inevitable gay grapevine. Several weeks passed and my meetings with Kelvin trickled to a halt. I met old friends less frequently and began to sense clouds of depression gathering on my horizon. Then, one night, as I was making my way to the Bandstand, I turned a corner and came face to face with one of my young colleagues. It was about 7.30 pm and as far as I knew he stayed home most evenings, so I was surprised to run into him.

'Vikas, fancy meeting you here!' I exclaimed.

As soon as I had spoken the words I realized how absurd

they sounded. He could well have said the same of me. He was a quietly spoken man, well groomed, and took pride in his appearance. Occasionally, he would let slip a coy smile but mostly he presented a serious demeanor. I had had little to do with him but found him pleasant to be around. When the Lavender League had played the game 'I wonder who else might be gay,' his name had come up as a possible candidate, but I'd dismissed it as speculation.

'I'm going to a movie at the Regal,' he said.

There were several cinemas in the vicinity so it was quite a plausible story.

'Oh, what's showing?'

I didn't mean to interrogate him but I was groping for ideas to keep words flowing between us. He hesitated, as if to come up with a suitable film title.

'Uh, *Mad Max II*, I think it is called.'

The Regal did show a lot of foreign films, but I couldn't imagine Vikas going for something as violent as *Mad Max*. It didn't seem to gel at all with his gentle manner.

'Well, enjoy the movie,' I said, as I waved him good-bye and proceeded to the Bandstand.

When I glanced back, he was progressing across the maidan towards the theater. A strange coincidence, I thought, to have run into Vikas in this part of the city at this time of night, but after my experiences in Delhi and Calcutta I'd come to expect such serendipitous encounters in India.

About a week later, I arrived at the Bandstand around 8 pm to find Akbar in a huddle with several others. As we chatted, I couldn't help scan the park for other faces that attracted my attention. So natural had this habit become that I sometimes didn't realize I was doing it. My eyes surveyed the crowd and came to rest on a figure on the other side of the rotunda. I blinked several times to confirm what I thought I had seen. Noticing I'd been distracted, Akbar broke in.

'Seen someone you fancy, have you?'

'Well, sort of,' I replied, 'but if I'm not mistaken, it's one of my own colleagues.'

Excusing myself, I started walking around the rotunda to the other side. I couldn't think fast enough to plan what to say, so I decided to go straight up to him and let instinct take its course.

'Hey Vikas, good to see you,' I exclaimed, trying to subdue my mixture of delight and surprise.

'Good to see you too,' he said.

'Do you come here often?'

'Not a lot. I only started coming a month or so ago.'

The young man sitting next to him stood up and began to move away.

'I'm sorry. I didn't mean to interrupt you,' I said.

'No problem. Please sit,' said Vikas.

This was not a conversation I had ever thought I would have and was certainly not one I was prepared for. I wanted to give Vikas a firm hug but not even gay men in India would dare do that publicly. How often I'd squirmed when one of our newly arrived foreign staff broke this basic rule of cultural etiquette. But words were hard to come by right now, even though I had dozens of questions. Vikas probably did too.

'How did you find out about this place?' I asked.

'I met a guy from the Navy Men's Hostel just down the

road. He told me about it.'

I'd heard rumors of sailors from the hostel frequenting the Bandstand, but to my disappointment I'd never met any. Vikas had, and from what he told me, he'd thoroughly enjoyed the experience.

'You know, when I ran into you on your way to the cinema, I had my doubts you were telling the truth.'

'Well, partly. I had arranged to meet my friend there. That's where we first met.'

Vikas's audacity and sense of adventure astonished me. There was more to him than I would have guessed from observing him at home and in the office. He had whetted my appetite and I couldn't wait to find out more. How long had he been conscious he was gay? Did he know if any of our other Indian colleagues were? Was he aware of the existence of the Lavender League? Did he know anything about this new disease affecting gay men? Although I found him attractive, I decided I would never make any sexual advances to him. He was like a younger brother and the line I had drawn between my personal and professional lives remained firmly intact. I felt quite avuncular towards him in a protective kind of way. I suggested we meet to have a good talk and he readily agreed.

Just then, I sensed both of us needed a chance to digest the enormity of what had just happened. I wasn't sure what was going through his mind but a major implosion had taken place in mine. After more than three and a half years of exploring all corners of this megalopolis and a number of other cities across this vast country in search of gay men, I had discovered one living and working under our own roof and who shared many of the same values and constraints. I wanted to jump up and down and scream out loud. In an odd way, all my nefarious undertakings now seemed strangely justified.

As keen as I was to talk further with Vikas, that wasn't possible right away, since I was about to go on another trip to Calcutta. But as soon as I returned to Bombay we settled for a glass of lassi at a local dairy shop. It became clear that Vikas had only recently begun to pursue his attraction to other young men. In this way, I was only a little more advanced in the game than he was, although a few years older, but he had a head start on me by about a dozen years.

As I spun for him the tale of my last few years, he listened with rapt attention. There were parts I skipped over and skirted around, since I didn't want to inundate him with too much too soon. He had no knowledge of the Lavender League but was eager to consider himself a part of it. Like me, he had assumed he was utterly alone in the organization in his quest to come to terms with his interest in his own sex. To have found someone with whom he could share his precious secret was a blessing he had never expected. I showed him articles and books that other League members had sent me and talked about our plans for meeting at our staff gathering in Chicago in eight months' time. Vikas said little, but nodded affirmatively.

When I realized how quickly time was passing and how little I had heard from him, I tossed the ball back into his court. I asked him if he knew of any other colleagues in India who were of our persuasion. He hesitated for a second, glancing first at the floor and then out into street.

'I don't think anybody else in Bombay is gay,' he said, 'at least among our Indian staff.' I was aware that he and other young Indian men took their morning bath together in one of our two small bathrooms. But I also knew that Indian men never bathed naked, preferring to cover themselves with their lungi or underwear while dousing themselves with water. If there had been moments when even a furtive glance had passed between them, he surely would have known.

'So, what about other places?' I asked.

'Well, there was someone once, in a village where I was assigned. You remember Wadgaon?'

How could I forget? It was one of the first villages where I had lived and worked in India, and the first in which I had been assigned as project director. The village boasted a proud Maratha heritage and caste still ruled with an iron fist. Hours of meetings with neighboring villages and endless trips with village leaders to the offices of government officials—even to the Chief Minister of Maharashtra—had consumed much of my stay in that village, with little to show for it at the end of it all.

But there was one recollection from that time that stayed with me. Among its population of several hundred were a number of young men who I had found exceptionally good looking, even before my heightened awareness of my own sexual inclinations. Coming from upper and middle castes, they would cavort together in the village, when not attending college. During the summer holidays, they would swim in one of the village wells, splashing around in their underwear that often revealed their proud manliness. When I had once accidentally stumbled upon them frolicking together, one of them invited me to join them, but at that time the call of duty had overruled such personal pleasures.

After my work in Wadgaon was over, I was replaced by a

Canadian, whose team Vikas was assigned to. As he sat across the table from me, one hand around the empty lassi glass and the other touching his chin, he told me something that caused my jaw to drop, partly in disbelief and partly out of envy.

'Did you know Joe was asked to leave Wadgaon?'

I confessed I didn't.

'He enjoyed with some of the young men in the village.'

I was touched by Vikas's quaint and succinct way of putting it. I was inclined to respond, 'God, how I wish I had, too!' but propriety got the better of me.

'So what happened exactly?'

'When word leaked out, there was a big fuss and the panchayat told him to leave the village.'

I recalled hearing that Joe had been reassigned to another village in mid-term but I had never asked why. I thought about the warm send-off I had been given, along with kind words and a silk shawl. While I felt sad about the manner of Joe's departure it also reaffirmed my decision to separate my personal life from my professional life, especially in villages.

I decided not to probe further, in spite of my deep desire to know more about Joe's activities and any possible part Vikas may have played in them. There would be opportunities later, I felt sure. I was pleased Vikas trusted me enough to share what he had, and I was concerned not to damage our budding relationship. I wanted to nurture it as best I could, while dealing with my own unfolding journey.

BRIDGING THE GAP

Early in 1983, I invited my mother to visit me in India. This was no spur-of-the-moment decision. The groundwork for it had been laid the previous year when Sir James and his wife had visited my mother in Perth on one of their treks to promote the exposition. They had presented her with a small gift from me and urged her strongly to consider visiting India while I was still there. I had also enlisted the support of one of her closest friends, who had been gently but persistently urging her to make the trip.

At 66 and in good health, my mother was still quite able to travel. Besides, while she had visited my sister's family in Canada several times, she had never paid a visit to me in the 12 years since I had left home. Granted, my peripatetic lifestyle and my participation in the Institute hadn't offered her much incentive. Moreover, unlike my sister, I had not married and presented her with any grandchildren to entice her to come. I had turned out to be a grievous disappointment compared to the son she imagined I would be. When my high school foreign languages teacher spun tales about my attending the national university and entering the Australian diplomatic corps, visions of my having a secure career and residing in fine quarters must have preyed on her susceptible imagination. My living on a dung floor in a mud hut in a poor Indian village would never have crossed her mind.

After my mother gave a tentative nod to my invitation, letters began to flow back and forth. We would have a little over two weeks together and all of India to spend them in. Even though I'd lived and worked in the country for over five years, I had never played tourist. Where to go, what to do, whom to meet in 16 days in India? The possibilities were endless, the choices paralyzing. As always, I erred on the side of too much. I wanted to give my mother a taste of both rural and urban life, of classical India and modern India, of friends and colleagues, of air travel and rail travel, of five-star luxury and village simplicity. I wrote to friends, visited travel agents, and read up on places I had never imagined I would visit. In this flurry of activity, one person was pivotal.

Anil was the middle-aged managing director of a chemical manufacturing company in Bombay who had supported our work in the villages. Along with his job came a spacious condominium in Bombay's exclusive Malabar Hill and a company guesthouse in Delhi, as well as a car and driver in both cities. He welcomed me to stay in his home whenever I wanted, use his company phone for international calls, and offered to carry packages back and forth between me and my mother on his visits to Australia. When he heard my mother was coming to India, he insisted we stay with him in Bombay and at his company's guesthouse in Delhi, as well as use his car and drivers. His only regret was that he would be in Australia visiting his family during the time of my mother's visit, so he would not have the pleasure of hosting her.

He also introduced me to his travel agent to handle our itinerary. After years of standing in long lines at railway ticket offices, it felt surreal to have someone handle all the details and present me with an envelope full of tickets. I no longer needed to pretend to be a tourist in order to qualify for the limited quota of reserved train seats; I was one.

Not everything, however, went quite so swimmingly. Since Kolhapur had been such a fertile place in my experience of India, I felt compelled to share it with my mother, both the village in which I had lived and worked, and the city where I had many wealthy friends. But getting there and back proved more difficult than I had imagined. The overnight bus trip, even on the so-called 'luxury' bus, would mean a sleepless night, while the train from Bombay had only one first-class carriage, and within that only one private compartment with closed doors. Known as the VIP suite, it was available for politicians and government officials at short notice. Meaning to give my mother a modicum of privacy, I made a temporary reservation three months in advance—only after 1 pm on the day of travel would I learn if we were to be the lucky occupants of the compartment.

As months rolled into weeks and then days, anticipation of my mother's visit kept rising until it began to consume me. I so much wanted it to be a success, for her as well as for me.

The day before she was to arrive, I moved from our staff quarters in the chaotic heart of old Bombay to Anil's grand home in leafy Malabar Hill, where guards stood at the entrance to private compounds and fruit-wallahs sold papayas and mangoes at three times the price paid for them at the market. With my mother's arrival in the early hours of the following morning, my sense of nervous anticipation peaked. That night, I hardly slept a wink.

What had started a year or so before as a vague idea was about to become reality. Memories of a dinner conversation with my mother in London four years earlier came flooding back. The psychic she had visited had been right. I would experience a major change in my life, but not the kind either of us could have conceived. Maybe this was to be my time of reckoning. How I wanted to share with my mother what had happened to me. But how painfully difficult, if not outright impossible, that seemed. For her, it was bad enough that I had joined such a nondescript organization for such ill-defined work, and with no pay. On top of that, to declare that I was gay might be too much for her to handle. I agonized over whether and how I should break this news to her. Sensing that my fate was in the lap of the gods, I made a small offering to the elephant-headed Ganesh enshrined in the front lobby just before leaving for the airport.

As I pushed my way through the crowd outside the arrivals hall, I nearly despaired when I discovered two flights from the Persian Gulf had landed shortly before my mother's. She would have to contend with hordes of returning Indians laden with enormous quantities of goods. I anxiously watched the exit door, as passenger after passenger came into view, pushing carts stashed high with boom boxes, television sets and towering mattresses. I visualized my mother collapsing in a corner of the giant arrivals hall and bursting into tears.

After more than 40 minutes, I could hardly believe my

eyes when she burst through the glass door into the steamy morning air. Wearing a loose-fitting, bright pink cotton dress, she was an easy target for the sea of self-appointed luggage carriers that was about to come crashing down upon her. Determined to beat them at their own game, I left Anil's driver at the barrier and raced towards her like a protective security guard shepherding a head of state.

'Hi Mum,' I yelled. 'You made it! Good to see you.'

'Yes, I made it,' she said in a self-congratulatory kind of way. 'But it would have taken me a lot longer if it hadn't been for a nice customs man back there. He didn't even bother to check my luggage. He led me to the front of the line and whisked me through. Crikey, it was a real zoo!'

I gave my mother's hand a gentle squeeze and kissed her right cheek, then guided her cart in the direction of our driver.

'Aren't we getting a taxi, John?'

'No, Mum. We don't need to. Anil has given us his car and driver while you are here.'

My mother had met Anil and appreciated his kindness. But carrying an occasional package was one thing. Offering your home, guesthouse, servants, car and driver for two weeks was quite another. I had a hunch my mother would take a little time adjusting to this pampering.

'I know this might feel a bit strange, Mum, but you'll have to get used to having people do things for you that you would normally do for yourself. But it won't last, so enjoy it while you can.'

'Oh, I'm sure I'll manage. It will be nice to have someone else doing things for me for a change.'

As we sped away from the terminal building it was a little

after 3.30 am. One advantage of arriving in Bombay in the early hours of the morning is that you are spared witnessing this urban monster arouse itself from restless sleep and drag its Leviathan body into another day. I was torn between the impulse to shield her from the harsh realities of India, and encouraging her to enjoy its unanticipated pleasures. However, managing such a balancing act stretched me to my limits. It was time for me to let go and allow the mystery to take charge.

I'd had quite a bit of practice at letting go these past few years, but something else was going on here. My mother had dared to step outside the safe confines of her tightly controlled world and enter the dramatically different universe in which I lived. For the first time in my life, I had a strong, instinctual urge to protect her and guide her through the maze she was negotiating—the puzzling customs, the confusing speech patterns, the unfamiliar tastes and smells, and the sharp contrast between the detached, impersonal way people often deal with you in public and the close bonds that one forges on a personal level. My greatest fear was that she would find it all too much and withdraw from the challenge.

Although we were both lacking sleep, the excitement of our pending adventure kept us wide awake. When Anil's servant, Rahul, welcomed us to our new abode with a pot of tea, any lingering doubt about taking a nap disappeared. As she stood on the balcony of Anil's apartment and looked out over the manicured garden below, the screeching of parakeets shattered the morning's tenuous calm. She could have been in a cameo of a Merchant Ivory film, surveying her private estate with matronly pleasure. I wondered what she was thinking as she tried to take in the new world she had burst in upon. I suspect she was pleasantly surprised by its luxuriant surroundings and deceptive serenity. Since our itinerary was filled to the brim, I had tried to leave this first day uncluttered to allow my mother to overcome jet lag and give us a chance to become reacquainted. I sketched out plans for our next two weeks and asked her if there was anything she would like to do. But she was content to let me decide everything, in the same way she had always relied upon my father to handle the details.

The overnight train ride to Kolhapur went without a hitch, although each time we stopped I was concerned some government official might board the train and demand our compartment. When we arrived in Kolhapur early the next morning, I searched the platform for our hosts, but couldn't see them. I was about to give my mother her first experience riding an auto-rickshaw, when a pale green Mercedes pulled up and out popped smiling Govind, a stocky young man with a chubby face. He extended his hand to me in welcome.

'Nice to see you again, John.'

Before I could introduce my mother, he turned to her and gestured with a brief namaste.

'Welcome to Kolhapur, Mrs. Burbidge.'

As a medical student, Govind had chosen to follow in his father's footsteps. Being an only child and son in a wealthy Indian family would not have been easy, since all expectations for personal and professional excellence would have been heaped upon his shoulders. But Govind seemed to take it all in his stride. He showed no signs of being spoilt and acted maturely for his age.

'Sorry I am late,' he apologized, 'but I had a little trouble with the car.'

Self-taught motor mechanics was another of Govind's skills that I would come to appreciate during our short time together. For the next several days, he acted as our host, guide, driver, shopping assistant and medical adviser. In a subtle way, he also acted as a buffer between my mother and his parents.

As we pulled up at the entrance of his family compound, the chowkidar rushed to open the gates to allow us through. The car had scarcely come to a halt when the door was opened for my mother by an attentive servant and Govind's parents presented themselves on the front steps. A confusion of namastes and limp handshakes followed, as often happens when Westerner meets Indian for the first time. I had primed my mother to refrain from handshakes and showed her how to do the traditional namaste instead. After this initial flurry of activity, we were ushered into the downstairs living room with its floor-to-ceiling windows that sucked in the brilliant morning light. Govind's mother whispered 'Chai, chai' to the kitchen staff, as our luggage was carried upstairs by one of the servants.

'So how was your trip down from Bombay?' asked Dr. Vasant, looking at my mother.

There was a momentary silence while she marshaled her words. I was about to come to her aid when she replied.

'It was very comfortable, thank you. We had a whole compartment to ourselves, which…'

'Ah, so you were lucky enough to get the VIP suite, eh!'

'Yes, I understand it took a bit of doing, but…'

'It can definitely take a bit of doing, with all this tomfoolery these politicians play. And where are you staying in Bombay?'

'A good friend of John's has given us the use of his beautiful home while he…'

'You know, my brother is in Bombay. You could stay with him and his family if you wish.'

After the preliminaries were over, Govind's mother, Mira, escorted us upstairs to the guest bedroom. It was about three times larger than the one my mother had left behind in Australia. I remembered the nights I had spent in this room while visiting from the village, and how difficult it was at first to reconcile its exorbitant space and comfort with the confined area and hard wooden floor on which I normally slept. Learning how to operate in both worlds and move effortlessly between them was another valuable lesson India had taught me.

Over the next several days we explored the city and its surrounds as we visited the former Maharajah's palace, drove to a nearby hill station, and were hosted by other friends in their homes. In contrast to Bombay and Delhi, Kolhapur operated at a less frantic pace that made it ideal to ease my mother into India and prepare her for what was to come. But most of all, I had chosen Kolhapur because of the nearby village where I had worked. Prior to our arrival, I had sent a telegram to our village staff to arrange for our visit. They were adept at hosting visitors but I had no idea how my mother would react. With Govind as our driver, we headed out early one morning on the 45-minute drive to the village. I had traveled this way many times, usually on a state transport bus and occasionally on the back of a motorcycle that belonged to one of the more affluent villagers. Never had I sat in the back of a chauffeur-driven Mercedes.

Word of our arrival spread fast. As we walked around the community, several elders joined our entourage and

'Namaskar Mr. John' echoed from doorways and windows. We stopped by the two-room school, the potter's house, the dairy cooperative and the flour mill, before coming to a halt at the brick-making factory run by the village's lowest caste. With sari-clad women and ponytailed young girls seated on the ground, my mother stood between me and the head of this impoverished community while Govind took our photo. The photograph shows a relaxed and confident mother smiling at the camera. Did she find my strange world not quite so intimidating after all? Was she even a little proud of what her wayward son had done? Years later, after she had moved to a nursing home, I came across this photograph. On the back she had written: 'The project where John first worked when he went to India…it is now entirely run by Indian folk.' I took this to be a ringing endorsement of my endeavors.

But our short stay in Kolhapur wasn't all accolades for me. On several occasions, I found myself in the hot seat, gently warmed by the courteous ways of Indian women. Both Mira and the wife of another doctor friend we visited decided to use my mother's visit to press their claims for me to marry. Marriage in India is not a matter of personal preference but carries a social obligation to not only ensure the continuation of the family line but to care for elders in their final years. That I was in my early thirties and had not yet married was incomprehensible and disturbing to my Indian friends. Mira, who was demure and soft-spoken, had started naming young women whom she considered suitable matches for someone committed to 'social work,' as she referred to my community development activities.

My mother had been asking about my intentions to marry

for some years but appeared to have resigned herself to what looked like a lost cause. Now she found reassurance in others who supported her position. The topic arose on several occasions during our stay in Kolhapur and each time I avoided making any commitment. At one point, Govind came to my rescue. Whether it was out of a sense of being in the same boat or whether he suspected my true sexual leanings, I never discovered.

'Give the guy a break,' he quipped. 'He can make his own decisions when he's ready. Besides, it's different in the West.'

Silence filled the void that his words had created. Mira stepped into the breach and steered the conversation to another topic, but not before berating her son for his outspokenness. I was grateful for Govind's bold stand, which appeared to have an effect, since the subject never came up again during the rest of our stay.

On our final night, after a mouth-watering feast of Kolhapuri specialties, we retired to the living room with several relatives who had joined us for the evening. Mira asked if my mother would like to listen to some ghazals. I felt it would be a chance for her to taste something new that probably wouldn't come again, so I gratefully accepted the offer. Mira produced her tamboura and sat down on a mat on the floor. After tuning the instrument and clearing her throat, she launched into her first piece. Her ululating voice filled the room, gathering momentum as she progressed. It may not have been music my mother understood or felt comfortable with, but Mira's virtuosity enraptured her.

The next day, before leaving for the station, I asked Govind to take me to the market so I could buy my mother a memento of Kolhapur to take back with her to Australia.

'I know the very thing,' he said. 'Come on.'

We jumped into the Mercedes and made straight for a store in the market that sold plaster statues of Indian women playing classical instruments. I picked out one that was small enough to fit comfortably in a corner of my mother's living room. When I presented her with it, she lit up like a small child opening a Christmas gift.

'It's so beautiful!' she exclaimed. 'And it is just like Mira played last night. It will always remind me of my wonderful visit to Kolhapur.'

I had the statue packaged in a box generously padded with straw. My mother guarded it carefully on the train to Bombay and sat it on her lap throughout the flight back to Australia. For her remaining years, it occupied a prime position on her dark red credenza, adding elegance to the room and often drawing comments from visitors.

'Yes, John bought me that when I went to India,' she would say, with a hint of pride in her voice. 'It comes from a place called Kolhapur.'

* * *

On our return to Bombay, I again asked my mother to let me know if there was something she would especially like to do, but she declined. However, there was one question she did ask from time to time: 'When are we going to visit the Institute?' I promised we would do it soon, although something kept me from making it a priority. An unexpected meeting with one of my coworkers at Nariman Point brought my delaying tactics to an end. Having her hair done was one of my mother's weekly rituals, so when she discovered the range of offerings of the Oberoi Hotel beauty salon, and their modest prices compared to those in Australia, she decided to treat herself to the whole palette—manicure, pedicure and hair. While I was waiting for her to emerge from the salon, I ran into Dorothy in the lobby. She asked how my mother's visit was going and invited us to join her and her husband for lunch one day. When I told her of my mother's interest in visiting our staff quarters, she suggested we all go back together in a taxi.

My mind flew into panic mode, since I had no idea what she would be walking into. I was most concerned about the state of my room, which I shared with a young German who must have been the only one of his countrymen born without the Germanic gene for orderliness. I had managed to keep the room tidy most of the time I had spent there, but since I had been away more than a week I suspected it would look like the aftermath of a hurricane.

I made a quick phone call to our residence and explained my dilemma to one of our American staff. He promised to make sure the room was presentable. When I returned Dorothy had been joined by my mother and they had struck up a conversation. Things seemed to be falling into place nicely.

Dorothy offered to act as guide to our staff quarters, but when it came to my own room I took over. As I walked through the curtained doorway my jaw dropped. Sprawled out on the lower bunk, dressed only in his underwear, was the sleeping form of one of our British colleagues. He must have just arrived in Bombay and crashed on the nearest bed. Or perhaps knowing I was away, someone had suggested he make use of my bed. The remainder of his clothes lay strewn over the floor and my desk was covered in papers, books and mail.

It was too late to take remedial action. My mother was hot on my heels and bristling to see this innermost sanctuary of my private life. I apologized for the mess but she acted unfazed by it. She made straight for the desk and honed in on the photograph my German roommate had displayed of his parents.

'You don't have any photos of your family, do you?' she commented.

Her simple statement caught me off guard and sent me spiraling downwards. I groped for something appropriate to say and found nothing suitable. The truth was, it had never occurred to me to display photos of my family. They felt so disconnected from my present life. My father had died 10 years before, my mother was emotionally distant, and my only sister lived a world away in Canada. Moreover, there was no one else in my life to whom I had any strong personal attachment. I did have snapshots of some of my favorite Indian friends but I wouldn't have dared display those. When I joined the Institute, it was as if I had entered a religious order and put all other ties on hold.

We adjourned to the front porch where Dorothy brought us tea and biscuits. As we sat there, I wondered what was going through my mother's mind. From the moment she got out of bed in the morning until she lay down again at night, she was exposed to a universe of difference that demanded responses from her. That could be quite draining and I tried to be sensitive to it. When she would ask a question or make a comment, I responded as honestly and accurately as I could. But there was one question I was not sure how I would handle. Part of me hoped we could avoid the subject as we had done for years. Another part desperately wanted to get it out on the table and deal with the consequences. I decided to let my mother make the first move.

The opportunity presented itself sooner than I could have guessed. After leaving the Institute, we took a taxi back to Malabar Hill. As we were waiting at an intersection for the lights to change, my mother looked out the window and noticed two young men holding hands. This wasn't the first time in India she had witnessed such a sight, but so far she had not commented on it. She turned towards me, screwed up her eyes, and posed the question.

'Are there many homosexuals in India, John?'

I struggled to find the words to respond. Was this an innocent question prompted by what she had just witnessed or was there more to it? Did she suspect I was gay but didn't know how to raise the issue? Either way, should or shouldn't I take this opportunity to broach the subject of my newfound sexual identity? How would she react? Things had been going well so far and I didn't want to risk tearing the delicate fabric that had begun to weave itself between us. Then again, we still had little more than a week, so there would be time to talk things through after my disclosure. So many imponderables. The stakes were so high.

'Oh, I guess there's probably about the same percentage of gay men in India as in most countries. Why do you ask?'

'Well, I've seen so many young men here, behaving, you know, like, well…young women do in Australia. Very friendly with each other, and in public too. Not quite what you'd expect, is it?'

'Well, Mum, it may not be quite what you'd expect in

Australia, but Indian customs are different. It's okay here for men to show affection for one another in public. And it doesn't mean they're homosexual, although some probably are.'

My mother looked confused as she mulled over my answer. Whatever was going on in her mind, she decided not to pursue the matter further at this point, and neither did I.

* * *

The remainder of my mother's stay in India was divided between Bombay and north India, with Anil's company guesthouse providing us with a comfortable base in New Delhi. Lavish temples, historical memorials and humongous government buildings lining expansive boulevards give New Delhi its distinctive flavor as the nation's capital. But it wasn't those grandiose icons that left their imprint on us during our week's stay. It was something much more personal. With the exposition less than six weeks away, our Delhi staff decided to celebrate all their hard work with a New Year's Eve party. Since we had no other plans for the evening, I decided to bring my mother along and introduce her to more of my coworkers.

Not long into the evening, one of our Delhi directors asked everyone to gather round to reflect on the past year and the one to come. Such activities were commonplace in our organization, but to those encountering them for the first time they could appear a little strange. I was concerned how my mother would react and wanted to spare her any embarrassment, but decided to let things take their course.

The questions themselves were innocuous enough, beginning with, 'What is something from this past year you are grateful for?' As the responses wound their way around the group, I could sense a rising apprehension in my mother as she kept changing the position of her hands on her lap. The unexpected demand to speak out in front of the whole group seemed to be crushing her. When her turn came, she remained silent. The young woman leading the conversation offered kindly prompts, but when these didn't help she suggested we move on and perhaps come back to my mother later. I labored over how to release my mother from the agony I sensed she was in.

Following the conversation, the group disintegrated into smaller circles, and food and drink were passed around. As the evening wore on, my mother loosened up a little. Several others made a point of chatting with her and she appeared to respond positively. Close to midnight, I noticed her locked in discussion with one of our Indian staff who had had more than his fair share of alcohol. My mother never drank anything stronger than a lemon squash, but she was holding her own as she went head to head with him. From across the room I picked up the drift of their conversation. My mother was on her usual hobby horse, deriding my decision to join the Institute in favor of a more secure and respectable job. My colleague was put in the position of defending me and the Institute. I decided to let them slog it out. My mother seemed visibly more relaxed, as opposed to her nervous, withdrawn stance a short while ago. I wasn't sure what had triggered the transformation, but was delighted it had happened. Perhaps India was working its magic on her too.

When I look at a photograph taken that evening, I marvel at what I see. It is a group of six of us—my mother, me and a young American coworker, a tall, vivacious-looking young

Indian man, Kavita, and my newfound gay ally, Vikas. Dressed in a light blue and white floral dress, my mother occupies the center of the picture, standing out from the others with her much fairer skin and broad, rounded face. Her hands rest on Vikas's left shoulder and my left hand on Kavita's; we both seem oblivious to the cultural taboos we are breaking. There is a sparkle in my mother's eyes that I have rarely seen. Mine seem to convey a sense of accomplishment at bringing together such diverse strands of my life, even if for the briefest moment.

Two days later, we were back in Bombay. On our way to the airport, I found myself mulling over conversations we'd had and thinking about those we hadn't. The question of whether to share the news of my sexual orientation was uppermost on my mind. But the thought of doing so and then sending her on her way to try to make sense of it all felt unfair, so I decided not to. It would be another five and a half years before the occasion to do so presented itself.

In hindsight, I may have been wise to postpone it. I was still recklessly experimenting and hadn't thought through the consequences of such an acknowledgement. Even during my mother's stay, I had found opportunities to slake my unquenchable thirst for young men. At the time, I had no compunction about lying so shamefully to my mother about my sudden disappearances, although I later asked myself how I could have been so brazen. If she hadn't suspected my interest in other men till now, she surely must have afterwards.

When we reached the airport, we found that the flight was delayed, which gave us ample time to talk. We reminisced over the last two weeks and I inquired more about the life she was returning to. Just as the first boarding call for her flight echoed across the departure lounge, she opened her purse and handed me an envelope. She often gave me gifts of cash, but always withheld them to the last moment. It was her way of saying thank you on her terms.

I was grateful for the money, but so much gladder about her decision to come to India. Not once did she dissolve into tears or chew me out over anything that displeased her. After a final embrace, I kissed her on the cheek and sent her on her way. Over the years, I had always been the one leaving and she the one left behind. For once, she had risked entering my strange universe, and had performed admirably.

As I watched her amble down the jetway, I noticed she was chatting to a fellow passenger and wondered what she could be saying. I have seen off hundreds of people at airports and I don't usually linger. But this time, I could not pull myself away from the terminal window, tears rolling down my face. When the plane finally took off, I jumped in a taxi and headed to a nearby restaurant. After selecting a discreet corner table, I ordered a bottle of Kingfisher beer and a plate of palak paneer, and cried. The chasm between us had closed a little.

THE END OF THE BEGINNING

5 February 1984 had come to assume an almost mythic status in the life of the Institute. Like athletes training for the Olympic Games, thousands of our staff and others had worked tirelessly for years preparing for this day. As hundreds of participants from around the world poured into the New Delhi auditorium for the official opening of the exposition, Indian television cameras panned the crowd, and *Voice of America* interviewed delegates. Next to the podium sat lean, old men in white dhotis and tangerine turbans alongside buxom West African women layered in garments of iridescent green and stinging yellow. These were not your average conferees, laden with degrees and high-sounding titles. They were mostly local people, many of whom had never possessed a passport or flown on a plane, and had come to share their stories and to learn from others how grassroots people can work together to improve their lot.

My primary role in this mammoth event lay in its preparation and follow-up, from raising funds and securing advocates to producing public relations materials and editing a book that distilled lessons learned from this four-year undertaking. During the 10 days of the event itself, I helped in small ways and joined in the opening and closing sessions, but some days and most evenings I found myself in the rare position of having time on my hands. I didn't need suggestions on how to make use of it. The low-cost, government-run hotel that housed our staff offered a convenient camouflage for my activities. For once, I did not feel that my every move was being scrutinized as it often was in our staff quarters. I relished the anonymity as I threw myself into exploring Delhi's gay underground.

At night I would venture out, usually beginning at Connaught Circus in the heart of the commercial district. But when I was feeling more adventurous, I would take an auto-rickshaw to Nehru Park near the diplomatic enclave in South Delhi. During the day, this popular park attracted family picnickers, weekend concerts and art events. At night, it transformed into a haven for courting couples, gay men, drug peddlers and others, including plainclothes police whose intimidation tactics were well known. But the park's 35 hectares of mini-hills and landscaped vegetation created an illusion of privacy that made it a beguiling place for gay men in search of quick sexual release. I had a number of encounters here, but always felt a sense of relief when I safely returned to my hotel. The thrill of the hunt was still as strong as ever but it was invariably accompanied by a lurking fear. I sometimes thought that the combined effect of my mother's visit and the exposition would divert me from my relentless drive for sexual discovery. But they appeared only to have upped the ante. I now had to see if I could keep all these plates spinning at once.

As the exposition drew to a close on 14 February, I felt as though a chapter of my life too had ended. So much energy had been spent, individually and collectively, over the previous four years gearing up for the gathering in India that its completion came as an anticlimax. The next phase of the project would include follow-up gatherings in different parts of the world, as well as extensive documentation. When I was invited to join our Calcutta staff to visit participating organizations in Nepal and Bangladesh, I jumped at the opportunity.

A few months later, I was to join the bulk of our India staff and head to Chicago to participate in the Institute's largest-ever gathering. For years we had put funds aside to bring together as many of our staff as possible for two months to engage in a massive social research project, followed by an assembly in which we would review our work and create long-term plans. Despite my initial ambivalence, I had resigned myself to the fact that once I left for Chicago, I probably would not return to India. Nevertheless, the thought of leaving distressed me. I couldn't imagine not being a part of India, now that India had become so much a part of me. Loosening these ties couldn't be easy. Unwittingly, my visits to Nepal and Bangladesh helped this process along.

I had another strong incentive to undertake this assignment. It provided me with one last trip to Calcutta and the chance to spend time with those with whom I had come to feel a close kinship. Ever since my dam-bursting conversation with Sandy, my relationship with her had strengthened and I now saw her as something akin to a trusted sister. We talked and joked and shared stories in ways I never dared with other colleagues. For the first time in India, I had found a friend, with no sexual overtones and no strings attached. Whenever we met, I felt like a bird that had just discovered its wings and savored the unimpeded sense of freedom that flying brings.

From Calcutta, we traveled to Dhaka, the capital of Bangladesh. My image of Bangladesh as a land of savage monsoons and incessant floods was reinforced as our aircraft approached the elevated runway at the country's major airport, surrounded by water as far as the eye could see. Driving in the city a couple of days later, we stopped at the General Post Office to send a telegram. I watched in horror as Sandy stepped out of the taxi and waded through knee-deep water to get to the steps of the GPO. As in India, even the most mundane tasks in Bangladesh could become huge logistical undertakings. But unlike India, Bangladesh was nowhere as self-reliant economically. Whereas its Goliath-like neighbor manufactured everything from matchsticks to spaceships, Bangladesh was heavily dependent on imported materials. The standing joke we learned in Dhaka was that the country's most thriving industry was foreign aid, with its attendant government bureaucracies, non-governmental organizations, research bodies and assorted middlemen.

While the days were taken up in visits to development organizations, evenings were mostly our own. Sandy and I had checked into a United Nations guesthouse that made our own crowded facilities in India look third rate. After dinner we'd usually part company to give each other time alone. By now, I had developed an acute ability to predict where to find other gay men in any city I visited. Dhaka was no exception.

I found a pleasant area near the center of the city with a canal running through it. Before long, I noticed a number of young men strolling up and down and eyeing one another furtively. As a foreigner I stood out from the crowd, so I decided to take a seat and see who would accept my subtle invitation. Within minutes, I was joined by an athletic young man who wasted no time getting to the point. As we chatted, he revealed that he had a foreign friend who worked for the French embassy and asked if I would like to meet him. My first reaction was to decline, since I had become so enamored with South Asian men that foreigners of lighter hues held little interest for me. However, given my short stay in Bangladesh, I thought the Frenchman might give me a useful perspective on the local scene. My young informer told me he would try to arrange a meeting with the Frenchman the following evening. Since the only way he could reach me was at the UN hostel, I gave him that contact information.

The next evening over dinner with Sandy I told her I was expecting company so would not be going out as usual. I waited for an hour, then two, but no one showed and no phone call came. Since it was my last night in Dhaka, I decided to give up and try my luck in the public domain. But it turned out to be a most unproductive evening. When I returned to the guesthouse, I found a note taped to my door. 'You had a late night caller. Tried to contact you, but no response. Tell you more over breakfast. Cheers, Sandy.'

Damn! So he had come after all. If only I'd had the patience to stay a bit longer. I couldn't wait to find out the details. What was he like? How was his manner? Was he my type? I had a hard time going to sleep, as I kept imagining scenarios of what might have happened. I was up as the first rays of sun splintered through the wooden blinds to announce another muggy day in Dhaka. I showered and dressed and headed downstairs to the dining room. I was the first there but after a few minutes Sandy joined me, her face aglow with a smirk that told me I was in for a thorough going-over.

'Well, you hit the mark this time, sonny Jim,' she said as she pulled her chair out from the table and sat down. 'All I can say is that you were lucky I'm your traveling companion on this trip and not anyone else.'

My stomach curled into a tight knot as I gave her a 'go on' look.

'About 9.45 last night, I was reading in my room when I got a call from the front desk. The guy on duty said there was someone to see Mr. John but that he couldn't raise you in your room. So I agreed to go down and see if I could deal with it. When I entered the lobby, the only person there was this young lad, who looked all of 16. I began to wonder what you'd been up to this time.'

Sandy's eyes twinkled as she spoke; clearly, she was enjoying this.

'Since you had hinted over dinner that you were expecting company, I assumed this was it, though I must admit I was imagining someone a little more...shall I say...mature? Anyhow, I introduced myself and asked him what he wanted. He didn't beat around the bush. He said, 'Please tell Mr. John I have arranged for him to meet Jean-Pierre tomorrow evening at 7 pm at the same place.'

'What could I say? I promised I would pass on the message but told him that unfortunately Mr. John would not be there tomorrow night since we were returning to Calcutta in the afternoon. I thanked him for his trouble and told him perhaps Mr. John could meet Jean-Pierre another time.'

I blushed as Sandy relayed what had taken place. She was absolutely right. Thank goodness it had been her and not Henry or one of our Indian staff last night. Sensing my embarrassment, she laughed as she turned away from me to the waiter standing nearby and ordered breakfast.

While this secret brought us even closer, it didn't remain a secret for long. On the flight back to Calcutta, she promised not to tell anyone—well, almost anyone. A couple of days later, over a beer in a local bar, Sandy's husband, Sean, turned to me with a wry smile that suggested I was about to be subjected to his Bostonian Irish humor.

'So Burbs, what's this I hear about your after-hours activities in Bangladesh? What do they call it, boating?'

'Well, close Sean. I think the word you are looking for is "cruising."'

'Ah yes, cruising,' he repeated. 'But somehow I think "boating" suits you better. Not quite so elegant. A little wider range of vessels, wouldn't you say?'

I smiled, raised my glass and said 'cheers.' From that day on, I was saddled with the title of 'the boatman.'

Following a short stay in Calcutta, I flew to Nepal with an Indian colleague, Gregory, to pursue avenues of cooperation with exposition delegates there. It was my first visit to this small Hindu kingdom sitting on the shoulders of India in the Himalayas and I wished I'd had more time to explore outside the capital. Gregory had been looking forward to the trip as well, since he had relatives in Kathmandu whom he had not seen in a long time. After a bumpy landing on the narrow airstrip nestled between high mountain peaks, we headed to the lodge we had booked near the heart of the city. Gregory's relatives had invited us to lunch the following Saturday. Having had several full days of appointments, we were glad to take up their offer. They served us an abundant meal of Nepali and Western food, so I decided to go for a walk and let Gregory and his relatives catch up on family gossip.

I had just turned the corner and begun walking down the street when I noticed a slim young man sitting on the steps of a house. I walked up and down the same street several times, before coming back to a building opposite him. I stared at him and he stared back. I decided to wait and see what would happen.

After several minutes, he waved me over and I sat down beside him.

'Why were you looking at me?' he asked.

I decided to lay most of my cards on the table.

'I find you very pleasing to look at,' I said.

My simple response had the desired effect. He soon revealed he had sex with guys, as well as women. He invited me inside his simple house and motioned me to lie down next to him. For about an hour we enjoyed pleasuring each other's bodies. All the time, I was worried someone might arrive unannounced, although my companion assured me no one would. I arranged for the young man to come to our guesthouse the following day when I knew Gregory would be out. After more than an hour of waiting for him, I gave up and decided to visit his house. When I arrived, I found it locked. I was just about to leave when one of Gregory's relatives came riding a bicycle around the corner. He was as surprised to see me as I was him. He asked me what I was doing there, so I told him I was visiting someone in the neighborhood. He looked at me askance. I prayed he wouldn't relay our conversation to Gregory, since I would have been hard put to come up with a satisfactory explanation. It was a close shave, one that reminded me again that my drive for instant sexual release was out of control. Perhaps it was fortunate I only had a few more weeks before heading to Chicago.

On our last morning in Kathmandu, I was reading the local paper over breakfast when a tiny article on an inside page caught my eye. It stated that after 30 June, Commonwealth citizens would need visas to stay in India. Unlike my American colleagues, I had never had to worry about immigration matters for the six years I had been in India. Now that era was coming to an end. I took this to be another sign that it was time for me to move on. Part of me wanted to cling to this place that had redefined my life; another part of me knew that would be senseless.

***

Now that my departure from India was imminent, I decided to leave the country on a high. Things I had wanted to do, but hadn't, became priorities. Invitations from friends to dinners, movies and plays became more frequent. Communications with members of the Lavender League intensified, as the talking paper we had been working on was refined and the prospect of meeting other members of the group loomed large. Each letter I received from Chicago revealed names of more men and women who had stepped out of the shadows and joined our ranks. The guessing game of 'who will be next' became a favorite pastime. My conversations with colleagues in India continued apace and responses were most affirmative.

For the first time, my life didn't seem to be moving along two separate tracks and I found myself trying purposefully to merge them into one. Over the last several months, our community had been exploring the diversity of religions, arts and culture that make up India's rich mosaic. I suggested we invite members of different groups to our weekly roundtables to share with us their particular traditions. Since I knew more local people than most of the rest of our staff combined, I was in a unique position to make this happen. One of the most memorable of these was a young Parsi friend, who agreed to speak to us about Zoroastrianism and the Parsi community.

I don't recall how I met Cyrus, but the more I came to know him, the more I enjoyed our friendship. Although he was gay, I was not attracted to him in the way I was to other young men. Like me, he was a late bloomer in the game, so we found more interest in sharing our sexual discoveries with each other than we did in having sex together. He was an accountant from a wealthy and conservative family and lived with his aging father. As a member of two of the most exclusive private clubs in Bombay, he kindly invited me as his guest on several occasions. I had no way of reciprocating his generosity but when I asked if he would be our guest one Thursday evening, he readily agreed. His audience sat spellbound as he spun stories of the Parsis' flight from persecution in Persia, discussed their central role in Bombay's growth as India's commercial and industrial powerhouse, and told of their devotion to fire as a purifying symbol in the cycle of life.

While Cyrus made quite an impact on our community with his presentation, another gay friend did so in a rather different way. We had met during my mother's visit, at an

English-language play in the auditorium of Bombay's elite girls' school, Sophia College. During intermission, as my mother and I were standing in the foyer sipping drinks, I automatically began scrutinizing the crowd for young men. My rotating radar came to a halt on a smart-looking young man near the other side of the room. Each time I looked in his direction, I found him looking in mine. I excused myself from my mother on the pretext of having spied an old friend and headed towards him. A quick chat revealed a common interest and he asked me to visit him at his hotel after the show. I told him I needed to take home my mother first, but promised I would try my best.

This turned out to be the first of many enjoyable evenings I spent with Rajesh over the next six months. Whenever he visited Bombay, we would go out for dinner and sometimes a show. On one occasion, he had tickets for Martin Sherman's play *Bent* and asked me to join him. Set in 1930s Germany, the play depicts the plight of gay men under Hitler's regime. Max and his lover Rudy are forced to flee Berlin after the SS discover and kill a gay officer in their apartment. The Gestapo arrest the two men and put them on a train bound for Dachau concentration camp. On the way, Rudy is beaten to death by the guards, so Max denies his sexual orientation, pretending instead to be a Jew because he believes his chances for survival will be better. In the camp, he befriends another gay man who refuses to hide his homosexuality, but pays the price when he is shot by camp guards. No longer able to deny his true identity, Max dons his dead friend's jacket with its distinctive pink triangle and commits suicide by running into an electric fence.

After the performance, Rajesh and I talked at length about the play and its significance for us as gay men. While having sex with other men in India did not expose one to the brutality of a concentration camp, it was still illegal and could result in imprisonment, a sizable fine, blackmail and other forms of harassment, not to mention the great shame it brought upon one's family and the risk of being rejected by them. An anti-sodomy law introduced by the British in 1861 had never been repealed and it would be another quarter of a century before it was, then only to face further legal challenges. Even if it had been repealed, gay men might still have suffered many of the same atrocities. For the next few days, I could think of nothing but this play. I was convinced it was no accident that Rajesh had come to Bombay and invited me to see it. For nearly four years, I had flung myself into what I had called an experiment 'to test my gay potential.' At first, I had dipped my toes in the water, then I had waded out from the shore, a little farther each time, and on occasions I had dived deep under the surface into murky waters. When I had come up for air, I only wanted to immerse myself back in the depths. I was aware that what I was doing was technically illegal, but I felt compelled to pursue it. Even though I had had my scrapes with the law and others who might do me harm, I had somehow managed to remain unscathed. But how much longer would my luck last?

Bent forced me to confront this issue and stirred many questions in my mind. For the first time, I had a broader historical context in which to place my own personal quest. What had started out as a private matter now took on much greater implications. How had different societies and cultures treated homosexuals throughout history? What caused some to act with repressive force and others to embrace it more humanely? Why did it take India to illuminate my true sexual identity, when my own upbringing in Australia did not? The questions kept coming and I read everything I could lay my hands on in my quest for answers. Unfortunately, little on the subject was available in India, although several newspapers and magazines had begun running stories on the presence and treatment of India's gay men. I relied heavily on materials others sent me and I devoured them voraciously. This constant flow of information, the impact of the play, and my own coming out began to have an effect on me. I felt driven to make some kind of public statement about homosexuality and its relationship to our community life. It was just a question of how and when. I didn't wish to undermine the carefully prepared statement the League was working on. As I pondered this matter, two opportunities presented themselves.

During our weekly staff celebration, one member would be asked to make a brief personal statement about something that had happened in his or her life and reflect on its significance. The week following the play, I was assigned this role. The chance was too good to pass up, but I needed to carefully think about how to broach the subject to such a mixed audience. All week I wrestled with this issue, torn between being too explicit and too defensive. I finally decided to present the issues raised in the play in terms of social justice and cultural diversity, and let my audience draw their own conclusions about my participation in such matters. A few might not connect the dots, but surely most would. For the first time, I publicly uttered the word 'homosexual,' embraced it positively, and chose to be identified as such. Like Max, I had finally donned my pink triangle. Since it was not customary to comment on these personal testimonies, I never could gauge the response to my statement, but from the rapt expressions on people's faces, I sensed that my remarks had made their point.

A few weeks later, another opportunity to share more of my life came my way. The Institute had developed a curriculum for cultural studies courses that focused on the major societal changes and paradigm shifts in our time. While we offered these courses publicly, we practiced doing them on ourselves first. On this occasion, I was asked to give a lecture on the change from rural to urban lifestyles in the 20th century. You were expected to follow an outline that existed for this talk, but the challenge was to make it come alive by using illustrations from your own life. I had done this before and often found it grueling. This time stories flowed and insights seeped through, without my having to wring them out of my life. The question was not what to say, but how to say it so it would have the greatest impact. Halfway through the lecture, I realized no one was shuffling their feet or doodling in their notebooks. I knew and they knew that I wasn't just making some intellectual statement about theoretical issues, but was speaking from the heart. After the lecture, several people made it known that they had appreciated my effort, especially my authenticity and honesty.

As the day of my departure from India grew closer, I found myself pondering my future. Where would I want to be reassigned, if I had the choice? Which countries and residential communities would be the most welcoming to openly gay staff? How would I like to contribute to the future of the organization and which roles was I most suited for? I had come a long way in the last four years, but other challenges now confronted me. Having one of the founders of the Lavender League on the global staffing commission was a blessing. I'd heard that two American women had requested to be assigned together as a couple the following year. Given the traditional nuclear-family bias of our organization, such a move would be unprecedented. Their courage only reinforced my own will to keep pursuing the path I was on. The idea of entering into a long-term relationship with another young man, especially within the context of our community, had never entered my mind. It had seemed so far-fetched as to be ridiculous. Now it no longer felt that way.

When the day came for me to leave for the United States, I could barely contain my feelings. Although I was sure I would find some pretext to come back to India, there was something painfully final about going to the airport and stepping on the Kuwait Airways flight to New York. If I hadn't been asked to chaperone a couple of dozen of our Indian staff, most of whom had never flown, I may well have been an emotional mess.

Fortunately, I had another well-seasoned Indian traveler for company on the long flight. Ajay was a member of our Indian board of directors, and I had known him for some years. He was a youngish man, a little on the heavy side, with an impish smile when he spoke. He ran a small construction business and had contributed much to our village projects, as well as to the organization in other ways. After a refueling stop in Kuwait, our plane headed west across southern Europe. Having finished our meal, we shared a couple of beers and let our conversation drift. I don't remember how the subject arose, but it was Ajay who brought it up.

'You know, I heard something the other day that I couldn't believe. Someone told me that Delia is gay. Is that true?'

Delia was a fellow Australian who had worked in India during the time I had. She and her husband were popular among the Indian staff and had significantly contributed to our work there. When her husband was elected to our international executive council, they had moved to Chicago. I had recently learned that she had had a relationship with another woman staff member, but I didn't know much.

'I don't know, Ajay, but I've heard the rumor too.'

'I would never have guessed, from what I knew of her. We were very good friends.'

I took a deep breath and replied, 'I hope you'll continue to be, Ajay. By the way, what would you think if I told you I was gay too?'

I could hardly believe I had made such a remark. Would I have dared utter this a few hours ago, back on the ground in India? There must be something about being confined in a plane together, midair, thousands of meters above the earth, that emboldens you to say things you would otherwise never disclose.

'I'd be really surprised, to tell you the truth,' he replied. 'But then again, I've never known any gay men or women. I've only heard stories about them and read an occasional article. Maybe you should tell me more.'

Over the next few hours, I shared with Ajay the outline of my journey over the last four years. Now and again he interjected, but mostly he listened. His quiet, affirming manner masked the shock that years later he told me he experienced that day as I related my tale. While I had revealed my story to a number of friends and colleagues over recent months, Ajay was the first Indian among them I had dared open up to. After the silent reception I received to my lecture from my Indian colleagues, I was nervous about doing so. I knew I was risking a lot, perhaps too much.

But risk was something I had grown accustomed to these last few years, even welcomed. True, it had led me down some dangerous and life-threatening paths and caused me to question whether I had become a victim of my addictive propensities. But it had also unlocked the chains of my fettered life and had liberated me from the constraints of my own upbringing. It was as if it had become my ally. Without it, I never would have bought that copy of *Sexology Today*, I never would have ventured that Sunday afternoon down to Chowpatty Beach, and I never would have experienced that moment when I responded to the call, 'maalish, maalish.'

AFTERWORD

Ever since the British introduced a law in 1861 to criminalize homosexuality, the practice had been illegal in India and was punishable by hefty fines and stiff prison terms, with accompanying bribery and blackmail, as well as physical and sexual abuse. Then, in July 2009, after strenuous efforts by gay and lesbian activists and their allies, the Delhi High Court ruled that the law—Section 377 of the Indian Penal code—was unconstitutional, because it infringed on a citizen's fundamental right to nondiscrimination. Finally, after nearly 150 years this colonial anachronism had been banished.

But like many social changes this one was fragile and short lived. In December 2013, the Supreme Court overturned the Delhi High Court decision, with near-unanimous support of conservative religious leaders. A public outcry against this about-face was equally vociferous. Among the many voices decrying it was that of 83-year old Leila Seth, a former Delhi High Court judge and state Chief Justice and the mother of one of India's best-known authors, Vikram Seth, who is gay. Not only did she condemn the judgement because it failed to appreciate the stigma it attached to gay people and their families but also because it claimed, erroneously, that it would only affect a minuscule proportion of the total population.

In January 2014, I returned to India to participate in the launch of the Indian edition of this book. It was 19 years since my last visit and 30 years since I had lived there. I had been in Delhi barely 24 hours when texted about a rally that would take place in two days' time on India's Republic Day. It would focus on the repeal of Section 377 and a large turnout was anticipated. Would my partner and I like to attend? It sounded like a good way to ground ourselves in the reality of India today and to learn firsthand of the efforts being made by gay men and women in India to secure their basic human rights.

When we showed up at the rally's starting point, police seemed to outnumber participants but we were assured that people would appear. And they did. A mix of men and women, young and not-so-young, bright, articulate and passionate about their cause. But we soon discovered this was much more than a demonstration against Section 377. It pulled together a broad coalition of groups representing all those marginalized by Indian society—the disabled, women against sexual violence, those who dare to marry across religion or caste, and many more. They had all come to protest their exclusion from the protection of the Indian constitution, which had been celebrated that very morning with a massive parade of military might and cultural splendor down Delhi's grand boulevard, Rajpath.

As the crowd of several hundred wound its way through the city's streets to the rally stage, my mind cast back to the story you have just read. The only gay men I knew I met in parks and gardens, on trains or buses, or through personal referrals secretly passed on from one to another. It was inconceivable to me then that such a public demonstration for gay rights could take place, that gay men and women would risk outing themselves in such a public way, and that they would join forces with others similarly oppressed. India had changed, or so it seemed. The passionate speeches made by civil society activists, writers and others exuded courage and conviction and inspired those present to fight for their rights as members of 'the world's largest democracy'. But democracies require constant vigilance and outspoken critics if they are to serve all their citizens. India's LGBT community knows this only too well, as the events this day testified.

My own story now assumed a new relevance.

Growing up in a predominantly homophobic Australia, I had never identified as a gay man. Family, societal and cultural factors militated against it. It took India, with its bewildering complexity and unique way of embracing 'the guest as a god'—not to mention its abundance of extremely good-looking young men—to open this shuttered window in my life. When it did, I discovered a whole new world, albeit a largely subterranean one. I also uncovered a part of my psyche that had lain dormant for years.

In writing *The Boatman*, I have been pushed to articulate what this story is really about and why I feel compelled to share it with others. Was it about sexual addiction? Was it about an adolescence I'd missed growing up in Australia? Was it about living a double life? Was it about immersion in another culture and the awakening that can bring? These were all elements of my story but none could claim to be paramount. *The Boatman* is, as one person noted, a multi-layered love story—my love for another culture, my passion for its young men, and my immersion in the work I did. It describes an internal journey of discovering, exploring and integrating homosexuality into my life, while I literally journey through the teeming landscape of India. The two happen simultaneously, but the latter made the former possible.

Memoirs can take a long time to write. Often an extensive gestation period is required before the author is ready to tell his or her story. In my case, this was 30 years, during which time I have been in a single relationship for more than 25 years and helped raise two children. As fate would have it, I have also become the grandparent of a child who is part Indian. These experiences and the maturation they have brought have allowed me to write about my time in India from a different vantage point.

Seated before a largely young, and perhaps gay, audience at the Delhi book launch, I felt challenged to connect with them. What did they think about this middle-aged foreigner who sat talking about how India had so dramatically changed his life? How did his story relate to them and their ongoing struggle to achieve equality before the law and acceptance by society? I have no doubt that Section 377 of the Indian Penal Code will be repealed one day, but it will take a massive and persistent effort to sway public opinion sufficiently for India's lawmakers to take the political risk needed. Telling our stories, individually and collectively, is a key step in this process. If my story can provide the impetus for others to tell theirs, publicly and proudly, then it will have been worthwhile.

ACKNOWLEDGMENTS

My first attempt to write about my life-changing experiences in India was published without my knowledge in an Australian magazine in 1987. I accidentally discovered this when I happened to visit a London bookstore and found a copy of the magazine just as I was walking out the door. Then, fourteen years ago, encouraged by a few kind souls and with the benefit of hindsight, I tried to write a more elaborate and reflective version in the form of a memoir. This has been a long and challenging journey, which I would never have completed, had it not been for a number of people who assisted me in various ways. Among those, I would like to acknowledge the following:

Dianne Highbridge, author and friend, who encouraged me to pursue this project and cheered me along the way; Shyam Selvadurai, whose South Asian novels entranced me, and who took the trouble to respond to my questions; Suzanne Sowinska, of Richard Hugo House (Seattle), who taught me how much I still had to learn about memoir writing and provided many useful clues; David Vann, author and creative writing teacher, whose own memoir touched me deeply and who helped me sort through some thorny issues;

Karyle Kramer, Taylor West and Patt Wilson of the Whidbey Island Writers Association, who provided the framework and support I needed to produce chapter after chapter, which they generously critiqued; Mary Lindberg and Barbara Sjoholm of the Author-Editor Clinic (Seattle), whose expertise helped me shape a raw manuscript into a saleable story; Tim Curnow, agent and literary consultant, who guided me through the unfamiliar waters of publishing; and to my former colleagues Duncan Holmes, Sheila Maguire and Bruce Williams, who shared parts of my journey and provided valuable feedback as I attempted to share it with others.

Most of all, I owe much to my good friend and esteemed playwright, Mahesh Dattani, who not only captivated me when we first met but has continued to put up with me ever since. Without him, this memoir would not have been published.

Australian-born John Burbidge has lived and worked in Belgium, Canada, India and the United States. For many years, he was communications director for an international NGO engaged in community and organizational development, before becoming an independent writer/editor. His articles on a variety of subjects have appeared in magazines, newspapers, periodicals and books in several countries. He has edited volumes on civil society, rural development and memoirs, and is the author of a biography of Australian writer, Gerald Glaskin. He lives with his husband in Washington State, USA.